Your Marriage
Has Real Possibilities

BIBLICAL PRINCIPLES
OF MARRIAGE

Your Marriage Has Real Possibilities

BIBLICAL PRINCIPLES OF MARRIAGE

Cyril J. Barber

and

Aldyth A. Barber

Foreword by Ray C. Stedman
Preface by H. Norman Wright

KREGEL PUBLICATIONS
Grand Rapids, Michigan 49501

Library of Congress Cataloging in Publication Data

Barber, Cyril J. and Aldyth A.
   Your Marriage Has Real Possibilities.

   Bibliography: p.
   Includes index.
   1. Marriage—Religious aspects—Christianity.
2. Marriage—Biblical teaching. I. Barber, Cyril J. and Aldyth A. II. Title.
BV835.B34 1984   646.7'8   83-25537
ISBN 0-8254-2249-3 (pbk.)

Printed in the United States of America.

For Our Sons
ALLAN and STEPHEN

CONTENTS

FOREWORD

In the face of widespread breakdown in true family life and the sky-rocketing rise of divorce rates, many books are appearing which seek to shed the light of Scriptural wisdom upon the thousands who long for biblical help in their marriage throes. Scores of these books deal very helpfully with the *teaching* of the Scriptures, both in the Old and the New Testaments, on marriage and divorce. But more than teaching is needed. Wise counselors know that truth never finds a real foothold in our lives until it is *modeled* for us.

It is just here that Cyril and Aldyth Barber's volume does something unique. They skillfully set before us the marriages of the patriarchs (Adam, Enoch, Noah, Abraham, Isaac and Jacob) as the models we need, both as encouragement and as warning. They blend together contemporary case-histories in failing marriages and patriarchal examples of the good and the bad in marriage. The patriarchs emerge as men of like passions with ourselves, and their women as flesh and blood replicas of modern wives.

The sections at the close of each chapter, headed *Interaction,* will prove extremely valuable to any individual or couple who seriously seeks to follow a biblical example in marriage. My hope and prayer is that this insightful view of biblical models will help many in the monumental crisis we face today.

Ray C. Stedman

PREFACE

A delightful and practical book is the best way to describe *Your Marriage Has Real Possibilities.* In the midst of many volumes written for married couples, there is a refreshing quality to this work by Cyril and Aldyth Barber. The analysis and insights derived from couples in the Bible will be welcomed by the reader, and the discussion questions lend an added benefit to a study of this work.

The book has been written in a very readable style, and it is far more biblical in its content than many others which have been completed before. These illustrations taken from the Scriptures are very relevant for married life today. This will be a welcome devotional and biblical study for couples.

H. Norman Wright

INTRODUCTION

Pray thee, take care, that tak'st my book in hand,
To read it well; that is to understand.
—Ben Johnson, *Epigram 1.*

Lloyd Saxton, in his book *The Individual, Marriage, and the Family* (1977), discusses the statistical improbability of a person finding the right mate. He takes six criteria—physical attractiveness, intelligence, concern for others, a sense of humor, the ability to maintain a conversation, and the capacity to enjoy life—and demonstrates mathematically that a person would have to meet 15,625 people before he or she found an individual possessing these requirements.

If, however, a heterosexual relationship is desired (i.e., with someone of the opposite sex that might lead to marriage), then the probability of finding a compatible counterpart is one in 31,250. And if other criteria are added (e.g., race, religion, personal maturity, income), then the possibility of finding one's ideal is even more staggering.

All of this does not nullify the fact that we should pray that God will lead us to the one of His choosing. It underscores the importance of being the right mate for the one we eventually marry.

Being something is more difficult than *doing,* and so some young people enter marriage intent on changing their wife or husband. They hope that by doing so they will achieve their ideal. Such individuals are doomed to fail, to bring unhappiness to others, and eventually to suffer from frustration, disillusionment and mounting resentment. Lamentably, they will probably add to the divorce statistics some time in the future.

A better way of establishing a home is to build a relationship with one's spouse on biblical models and then, as two fallible people, work on developing true maturity, unity and sexual compatibility. In this way the marital problems which all experience may be prevented from becoming full-blown predicaments.

Your Marriage Has Real Possibilities is designed to provide a few biblical models—some to emulate, some to avoid. It is based on the Book of Genesis—the one book of the Bible which deals with the beginnings of life, marriage and the family. It had its origin in 1973 when I was asked to teach a couples class in a local church. The class had expressed its dissatisfaction with the course content found in their curriculum materials, and they had asked for a change.

The invitation extended to me necessitated that, in concert with those in the class, we develop a special curriculum that would meet their needs.

During the three years I had the privilege of teaching this class, we covered a variety of topics. Specific books of the Bible were studied as well as Bible doctrine. None of the topics treated, however, produced the same response as the course on "Couples in the Bible" with which we began.

A few years later, after having completed doctoral studies in marriage and family ministries, and being faced with the challenge of a dissertation, I decided to resurrect my notes, rewrite the material, teach it again, and in a more scientific fashion determine if marital enrichment could be achieved through the church. By using a battery of scientifically verifiable tests and a control group, I was able to assess the impact of the material on the couples who took the course. In a post-test it was learned that there had been a 70 percent improvement in the marriages of those present during the 13 weeks.

The results of this experiment were later published by Xerox University Microfilms under the title "Marriage Enrichment in the Church."

A work of this nature cannot possibly be produced without the help of other people. Therefore I would like to thank the Dean and the faculty of the Talbot Theological Seminary for kindly granting me permission to publish this material (Appendix E) from my dissertation.

Special thanks is due Professor Henry W. Holloman, Th.D., who served as my advisor throughout the entire project and whose encouragement will long be remembered.

Thanks is also due the Reverend J. Daniel Baumann, Th.D., director of the doctoral studies program and Professor Glenn F. O'Neal, Ph.D., Dean of the Seminary, for their many kindnesses.

I would also like to acknowledge the unfailing help of my dear wife, Aldyth. As I prepared to teach this material, she readily discussed with me a woman's perspective of the events mentioned in the Book of Genesis, and I am happy to have her name joined with mine in the publication of this book.

I would also like to express my sincere appreciation to Dr. Ray C. Stedman, senior pastor of the Peninsula Bible Church, Palo Alto, California, for so kindly reading the manuscript and writing the Foreword. In addition, I would like to thank Professor H. Norman Wright of Biola University and a licensed marriage, family and child counselor, for so graciously supplying the Preface.

Finally, I would like to thank my dear friend Mrs. Dan (Alberta) Smith for her excellent work in preparing the manuscript for publication.

As this book is published, Aldyth and I trust that it will help to (1) prevent marital problems from developing into predicaments; (2) cement relationships; (3) increase each couple's happiness, and (4) create a strong environment in which a couple may rear their children.

CYRIL J. BARBER

Hacienda Heights, California

1

WEDDING BELLS IN EDEN

Successful marriage is always a triangle:
a man, a woman, and God.
                                    —T. Cecil Myers

Genesis 1:26—2:25

The ancient Greeks observed the never-ending cycle of man seeking for a mate and looked for an explanation. They propounded the theory that at one time mankind had been perfect. Each person was complete, being both male and female at the same time. In this state they became proud and incurred the anger of the gods. For their sin they were separated from one another and scattered over the whole earth. Ever since then each person has been seeking the other, for without a mate neither is complete.

Millennia before these early students of human behavior began trying to explain mankind's innate desire for companionship, God had said, *"It is not good for man to be alone."* He therefore made woman and, when He brought her to man, laid His seal of approval on their union.

But marriage has fallen on hard times. It seems as if everyone from raconteurs to social scientists has joined hands in portraying its shortcomings and predicting its demise. Quite recently some junior high school students were talking about marriage. One member of the group seemed to favor the idea. A friend had noticed his interest in a girl in his class and warned, "Be careful, Johnny, puppy love can lead to a dog's life on a split level."

As young people grow older the same friendly banter continues. High schoolers will caution those who are "going steady" that "marriage is a proposition ending in a sentence." And before a wedding they will jokingly remind the groom that "the honeymoon is only the interval between the man's *'I do'* and his wife's *'You'd better'*."

Even the sages have their word of counsel. "Let your wife know from the start who's boss," they advise; "it's no use kidding yourself." And some will consolingly remind the happy couple that "marriage is like a violin: after the music the strings are still attached."

Whereas the jesting of one's friends is good natured and does not prevent anyone from making the most of married life, some modern sociologists see things differently. Citing all sorts of statistics, they tell us that "traditional concepts about marriage, love, and fidelity are as outmoded as the horse and buggy," and that the "mold" into which a "conventional marriage squeezes a person has its contours determined by long outdated social mores." They also decry unity within the husband-wife relationship and predict that those who are "hooked on togetherness" will eventually lack fulfillment in their lives and suffer the consequences of their stagnant personalities.

After biasing our minds towards their point of view by their literary sleight of hand, they add the *coup de grâce* to their argument by saying that "in marriage a woman settles for second best. She becomes 'just a housewife.' Marriage programs her for dependency, and her enforced submission to her husband's authority is tacit admission of her inferiority."

In spite of these ominous warnings more than ninety percent of all people marry. But with such predictions of inevitable unhappiness it isn't surprising that so many marriages fail.[1]

The question naturally arises, Is there any hope for marriage? On what basis may a couple establish a lasting relationship? How may they cultivate healthy interaction? And where may they find a workable plan for their lives that will include the rearing of their children?

To answer these questions we must begin at the beginning, in Eden. This is hard for us to do because our primeval parents were far removed from the world in which we live today. In their pristine state they had no knowledge of sin either by experience or observation, and were not distracted by worries of the past or concerns about the future. They had no financial pressures, interference from in-laws, or doubts about their respective roles, to hinder their personal growth or the pursuit of happiness.

CELEBRATION OF LIFE

To properly understand the situation Adam and Eve found themselves in, we need to examine carefully their origin and relationship to one another. As we read the first chapter of Genesis we are taken back to the earth's creation. There we are able to overhear, as it were, the counsels of the Godhead. *"Let us make man in Our image, according to Our likeness; and let them have dominion over the earth . . . And God created the man* [Adam] *in His image, in the image of God He created him; male and female He created them."* [2]

While the text mentions both *male* and *female,* only Adam was created at this time. As we know, later on Eve was made from a rib taken from Adam's side. She was, nevertheless, conceptually "in Adam" from the very beginning, and the events of this first chapter anticipate the fuller explanation found in Genesis 2:21-22. [3]

The importance of this fact to us is that both Adam and Eve were created in the image of God. This gave them a common dignity. As persons they shared equally the attributes of personality. Adam was not inferior to Eve, nor was Eve inferior to Adam. And in sharing the divine image they were able to enjoy a unique privilege—fellowship with God and with one another.

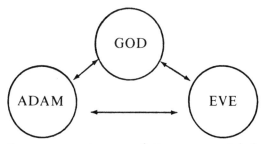

What then are we to say of the supposed inferiority of women? Is there any validity to the statement of John Stuart Mill that a "woman needs security and marriage guarantees it; man needs love and woman provides it; man is to command and woman to obey; this is the eternal principle underlying the relationships between the two sexes"? Is it true that "religion has been for women the single most iniquitous force in history"? Does there exist a worldwide sexual caste system masked by sex-role segregation?

In confronting these issues it should be pointed out that God created the first man and woman *in His image.* Ever since then men and women have shared equality as persons. Neither one is inferior to the other. It is tragically true, however, that in many false religions and in pagan philosophies the dignity of womanhood has been degraded. In the teaching of the Old and New Testaments, however, woman has been accorded her highest place. Unfortunately, man-made *traditions* have crept in and, in many cultures, have reduced the status of woman to little better than that of a slave. This is why Herbert Spencer could say "in the history of humanity the saddest part concerns the treatment of women."

In pursuing the biblical teaching, it is interesting to notice that in Genesis 1 the man and the woman are seen in relationship to their Creator. They are equal in His sight. In the second chapter the man and the woman are seen in relation to one another. Neither is complete without the other. In the union of their respective personalities, Adam loved his wife because she was everything he could wish for. Eve loved her husband because he was everything she needed. And together they enjoyed one another's companionship and shared dominion over the creatures of God's creation.

THE WAY IT WAS

In planning a wife for Adam, God shows that it is His general intention for people to marry. The events described in chapter 2 happened on the sixth day of creation and enlarge our understanding of God's plan and purpose for mankind. *"It is not good for man to be alone,"* He affirmed. *"I will make a helper suited* [i.e., corresponding to] *him."* The Bible then explains how God made Adam aware of his need. *"Out of the ground the LORD God had formed every beast of the field and every bird of the heavens. And He brought them to the man to see what he would call them; and whatever the man called a living creature, that was its name. And the man gave names to all the cattle, and to all the birds of the heavens, and to every beast of the field, but for Adam there was not found a suitable helper."*

In the naming of the animals we see something of the first man's remarkable intelligence. Not only has he been created mature in body, but his mind is developed as well. In naming the animals Adam assigns to them a name in keeping with a characteristic inherent in their creation.[4] In the process, however, he becomes aware of his aloneness. The animals pass before him in pairs, but no mate corresponding to him is found among the creatures of the earth. He alone lacks his complement.

But God does not make Adam aware of his need without planning to meet it. He causes a deep sleep to fall on him and, after opening Adam's side, takes from him a rib. From this He fashions the woman who is to be man's helpmeet.

The fact that Eve was created from Adam's side led Augustine to comment:

> If God meant woman to rule over man, He would have taken her out of Adam's head. Had He designed her to be his slave, from his feet. But God took woman out of man's side, for He made her to be a helpmate and an equal to him.

When God brings Eve to Adam he welcomes her and gives expression to the first love lyric in all of recorded history:

> **This, this at last, is bone of my bones,**
> **And flesh of my flesh:**
> **This [one] shall be called Woman,**
> **For from man she was taken.**

Adam's glad acceptance of the woman God has made for him forms the basis of their relationship. His joyous exclamation provides us with a beautiful and unvarnished description of his recognition of their oneness. They are ideally suited to each other. Eve lacks no charm and is attractive to Adam's sight. She is arrayed in all human perfection, is radiant in her loveliness, beautiful of form, and with intelligence equal to his. She is an ideal counterpart answering to his every need.

"And they were both naked and were not ashamed." The Bible discreetly draws a veil over their union in the garden. Sufficient for us to know that sex is God's idea (Gen. 1:28). Being free from sin, Adam and Eve can follow their instincts without fear. They do not need a manual on "explicit sex" to guide them and can enjoy each other without embarrassment. To them, sex is a beautiful blending of their persons.

PATTERN AND PROCESS

It seems as if there is innately within us the desire to be as Adam and Eve were when God created them. All of us at one time or another have entertained the fantasy of living somewhere, perhaps on a deserted tropical island, far removed from the pressures and frustrations of modern life.

What we long for in these unrealized daydreams is the kind of blissful perfection our first parents enjoyed. While this can never be true of us because sin has entered the picture, marriage still holds the greatest potential for joy and happiness. It can transcend all other human relationships. Unfortunately, when a husband or a wife treats the other person as a *thing* instead of a person of worth, their marriage either ends in tragedy or continues in misery.

THE STRUGGLE FOR EQUALITY

In our day there is a resurgence of interest in the equality of men and women. In the redefining of roles within the marital relationship, those who espouse the cause of women are in danger of pushing things to an unwarranted extreme. In the feminist movement women are striving to become like men. They are denying their God-given natural instincts in favor of acquired masculine characteristics. According to one woman physician, this has resulted in "hideous masculoid types who are bitter, self-obsessed, and steel-hard . . . They have degraded their fertility, publicly trivialized their sex, and now glory in their ex-female characteristics. Unfortunately for them, they suffer more than they realize. And with the accompanying demise of family life, the ideals of chastity, fidelity, fortitude, and self-denial are no longer being respected in the context of love."

This is a far cry from what God intended. God gave a woman a separate identity from a man and her greatest happiness comes through fulfilling the role He assigned to her. Success in marriage does not come merely through finding the right mate but in being the right mate. And this involves a woman being warm, affectionate, tender, and responsive, and a man being strong, compassionate, a good protector and lover. These are the characteristics that will draw from the other the quickest response and lead to lasting companionship. Marriage was designed by God to be a duet (not two solo performances). Both bass and treble clefs are necessary. To be sure there will be some discordant notes, but with mutual love, patience, and understanding, and with a willingness to make adjustments, a couple can develop true, lasting harmony.

THE STRUCTURE OF HARMONY

Apart from the essential equality of a man and a woman, what is needed to make a marriage succeed? A couple today is exposed to a thousand trials and temptations, delays and uncertainties, searchings and yearnings, which were unknown to the first pair. Are there any practical lessons to be drawn from this historic account?

Adam placed his finger on the three major areas of contention in marriage when he said, *"For this cause a man shall leave his father and his mother* [the need for maturity], *and shall cleave to his wife* [the need for unity]; *and they shall become one flesh* [the need for sexual fulfillment]" (Gen. 2:24).

At the very foundation of a marital relationship there must be commitment on the part of the couple to live together in a unique and lasting relationship.[5] The biblical teaching on marriage implies that marriage is for life (Mark 8:9). God looks upon marriage as a covenant (Mal. 2:14-15) and to break this covenant is to violate a sacred commitment. The uniqueness and permanence of this relationship is further underscored in the New Testament because marriage is used as an illustration of the relationship between Christ and His Church (Eph. 5:20-33).

One of the most crucial dimensions of marital counseling is in the area of *immaturity*.

Soon after we were married we began a Bible study in our home. One evening a young woman from our discussion group came to see us. She was very upset. She had recently learned that she was pregnant, and instead of being overjoyed found that her condition had precipitated a crisis.

When she and her husband were first married, everything seemed perfect. After a while, however, she found that he would never take action unless he had first discussed matters with his parents. This happened even after they had reached a joint decision on what should be done. Now that their child was on the way, the interference from her in-laws had reached an all-time high. She felt very depressed and did not know what to do.

Experiences of this nature are all too common, and their root cause is immaturity. Immaturity shows itself in many ways, such as being overly sensitive to criticism, or so perfectionistic that we become absorbed with the achievement of our ideals and fail to communicate with one another. And immaturity may also be seen in outbursts of temper or aggressive behavior, failure to assume responsibility in the home, and even in a husband's leaving the disciplining of the children to his wife. And then there are some who expect their wives to mother them.

Wives, on the other hand, may show their immaturity by their frequent visits "home," or, when they fail to find what they are seeking in marriage, complain that their husband's don't love them enough. And others, due to an improper example set them by their own mothers, may not know how to be warm and responsive.

These and many other factors are symptomatic of immaturity and account for the failure of many marriages in the first few years.

The second important principle of marriage is *unity*.

An elderly couple once shared with us how they first became aware of their own lack of unity. They had been married for twenty-eight years. Their two sons were married and living in adjoining states, and their only daughter had just left for college. On the evening of her departure, they sat at the table staring at each other. They had nothing in common. The only "family activities" had revolved around their children. And now that their children were gone, they had nothing to keep them together.

It is to their credit that they began to develop common interests—taking an active part in their church, going to art shows and social functions together, cultivating friends, and purposefully doing things together. But how tragic to wait until more than half of life is past before discovering the real blessing of proper union.

Psychologists have found that when "incompatibility" develops between a husband and his wife it is invariably traceable to a failure to understand the importance of unity. In the marital relationship, a husband and wife have separate roles. This does not destroy their unity but rather enhances it as each supplies what the other lacks. Unity, however, can only be developed by proper communication. This involves keeping in close touch with each other's hopes and fears, successes and frustrations. It means watching the small danger signals, taking note of facial expressions, and becoming sensitive to the other person's unspoken thoughts. It means caring about each other in tender and loving ways, knowing their faults and foibles, and recognizing *all* the good there is in the other person. It also means being deeply involved and honest with each other, whether the subject be an important one or not.

The development of unity is imperative if a marriage is to survive. Social pressures are such that disunity has become the order of the day. To combat these pressures, a husband and wife need to live together in a relationship which continues to develop and mature. For proper maturation to take place both parties need to have properly developed identities. Then with wholesome views of their roles, they can concentrate on the deepening of their relationship. As mature people they can handle outside interference and work towards common goals and ideals.

When problems arise due to immaturity or lack of unity, they are felt sooner or later in the failure of the couple to enjoy proper sexual fulfillment. This fact is borne out by psychologists who affirm that the third most important aspect of marriage is *sexual union.*

A few years ago we had the privilege of ministering at a camp for Christian couples. One evening a young man and his wife came to our cabin. He was very upset and began to unburden himself to us. He and his wife had been married for almost a year. At first their sex life was exhilarating. For the past few months, however, there had been an alarming deterioration in their sexual relationship. During the conversation we learned that the young man's mother, in attempting to warn him of the dangers of promiscuous behavior, had instilled in him the idea that sex was evil—"a part of one's lower nature." When once the newness of intimacy with his wife wore off, these old inhibitions began to reassert themselves.

As we shared with him the biblical teaching, he became aware of the fact that God is the Originator of sex. There still remained, however, the inner conflict between the way he had been reared and the new teaching he had received. While he and his wife left us confident that a new era was dawning for them, we all knew that it would be many months before the teaching of the Word of God would completely liberate him from his former inhibitions.

Tension over sexual problems also arises where either the husband or the wife has "played the field" before marriage. Their expectations may be higher and they may be quite unaware of the unexpressed resentment the other feels. They may also be repressing guilt over their previous liaisons. These suppressed feelings may now be hindering the full enjoyment of all that God intended.

Other areas of sexual maladjustment occur when a husband or wife engages in "sexual politics" and deprives their spouse of sex until they get their way (comp. 1 Cor. 7:3-5). Such "punitive" attitudes can only hinder the full development of a marriage.

God's pattern for a happy, fulfilling relationship is based upon the commitment of a couple to live together in a unique and lasting relationship.[6] The blessings of a healthy marriage (based upon Genesis 2:24) are that it makes our ideals an everyday possibility. These ideals can be achieved as we work together to bring about greater personal maturity, develop true unity, and share in the intimacies God intended us to enjoy.

Interaction

1. The first marriage was a "holy triangle"—God, Adam and Eve. Explore together the ways in which fellowship with God (a) enhances our relationship with one another, and (b) helps us overcome some of the trials and difficulties we all encounter. What is involved? How is such fellowship maintained?

2. In Genesis 1:27 the *fact* of man's creation by God is emphasized. Why does God give us this summary of what happened (vv. 26-28) before describing the *process* (Gen. 2:7, 18-25)? What significance does this have to us today?

3. In Genesis 2:15 man is told *"to keep"* (Heb. *shamar,* "to watch, to guard") the garden. Why? Does this indicate that God may have warned Adam and Eve of Satan's fall and activity? Should we, in a similar way, "guard" our homes? And if so, from what?

4. Before sin entered the world, Adam and Eve were given work to do. What does this tell us about (a) the nature, and (b) necessity of work? How may this change our attitude towards our "secular" occupations?

5. In Genesis 2:16-17 Adam and Eve are given a prohibition. How far-reaching is the restriction placed on them? Why is a test necessary? What is the difference between their state of innocence and being righteous?

2

OPPOSING VOICES

Morality, like art, consists in
drawing the line somewhere.
                    —G.K. Chesterton

Genesis 3

In the book of Genesis we have the record of creation, the beginning of the family, and the entrance of evil into the world.

The ancient philosophers looked about them and took note of the passions that stir the worst instincts in the hearts of men. They began speculating on their origin, and from their musing came the story of Pandora.

The gods of Mt. Olympus, so the story goes, had placed all forms of harm and mischief in a box and had committed the keeping of this box to Epimetheus. In the course of time Pandora was given to Epimetheus in marriage. She was a beautiful and gracious woman, and was in every way an ideal wife. She had only one weakness—an insatiable curiosity. She wanted to know what was in the box and, in spite of repeated warnings, one day lifted the lid. Out flew evil spirits of every kind which ever since have brought sorrow, grief, and misfortune to mankind. On seeing these spirits escape, Pandora clapped the lid down, but too late. The demons were gone. One good thing, however, remained—*Hope*. And Hope, so the ancients said, remains the sole comfort of man to this day.

FACTS AND FUTURES

In contrast to the obviously fictional character of the story of Pandora, the Bible explains how sin entered the world.

Critics of the Bible who have variously discarded Genesis 3 as mythological or legendary have done so because they wish to explain the fact of evil in more acceptable terms. Their efforts to avoid the unpleasant facts associated with their own depravity fail to account for the universality of sin. Inasmuch as other portions of God's inspired revelation treat this chapter as historical (see Matt. 19:3-6; Luke 3:38; Rom. 5:12-21; Jude 1:14; etc.), there is no valid reason for doubting that what is revealed in the Bible took place in any other way.

The question, however, has frequently been asked, Why did God allow the devil to tempt Adam and Eve? The answer must be found in the nature of God. He made Adam and Eve free from sin. They were in a state of untried innocence. This is different from being righteous. Righteousness could only be imputed to them after they had withstood a test. God desires only those acts to count as being of moral worth which freely acknowledge His sovereignty. In a test there must be the possibility of doing otherwise. To do what God desires solely because one has no alternative is of no moral value. Had Adam and Eve withstood Satan's temptation, God would have confirmed them in a state of righteousness.[1]

EVIL IN WAITING

No indication is given of the length of time Adam and Eve were able to enjoy their garden home. From their age when Seth is born (Gen. 5:3), and allowing for Cain and Abel to reach maturity, it must have been quite a long time—certainly long enough for Satan to study their situation thoroughly before making his move. As he observes them in the Garden he sees that they are perfectly content with all that God has given them. They have work to do (Gen. 2:15) and this keeps them from being idle. And the fact that God has commissioned them to *"keep"* (i.e., guard) the Garden seems to indicate that He has warned them of their adversary and his devices. Furthermore, as Adam and Eve meet with God in the cool (lit., the "breeze time") of the day and fellowship with Him, they have the opportunity to grow in understanding.

One particular day, while Adam is busy and Eve is near the tree in the middle of the Garden, the devil takes possession of the body of a snake[2] and approaches her. In all probability

Eve has seen this serpent before, but is caught off guard when it speaks to her.

But why does Satan approach Eve? Why not Adam, or both of them together?

Quite obviously, if Adam and Eve had been approached together the one would have strengthened and supported the other, and Satan's chances of success would have been greatly reduced. Some writers believe that the devil did not approach Adam because he knew that, had Adam yielded to temptation, he would not have been able to persuade his wife to follow him in his disobedience.

In all probability Satan singled out Eve, because he had observed the power she had over her husband. He had also noticed that she was less assertive than Adam and, not having heard God's explicit command herself (Gen. 2:16, 17), may have been less inclined to attach to it the importance it deserved. And then there is also the possibility that, in her growth towards personal maturity, Eve may not have developed as quickly as Adam. In less mature people the locus of control is external rather than internal, and in Eve's responses to Satan's subtle suggestions she exhibits quite clearly an external orientation (Gen. 3:6).

The entire account of the temptation of Eve is recorded with such brevity and simplicity that we need to analyze it carefully if we are to find out how the devil was able to motivate her to take the forbidden fruit. In all probability Satan approaches Eve as she is preparing a meal in sight of the tree of the knowledge of good and evil. He opens the conversation with a question: *"Is it really true that God[3] has said, 'You shall not eat from any tree of the Garden'?"*

Eve's reply is revealing. *"From the fruit of the trees of the Garden we may eat; but from the fruit[4] of the tree which is in the middle of the Garden, God has said: 'You may not eat from it or touch it, lest you die.' "*

In saying this Eve shows how she has fallen into Satan's subtle trap. He had asked a question which implied that restrictions are evil. Eve should have denied the charge (cf. Gen. 1:29). Instead she minimizes God's goodness (note the omission of the word *"all"*; Gen. 2:17) and enlarges upon His earlier prohibition by stating that even touching the tree will cause death. As a result she leaves herself open to Satan's renewed attack. She will soon discover, however, that the devil is never more dangerous than when he professes to be a well-wisher, interested in nothing other than a person's advancement or welfare.

Satan's response to Eve's vacillation is to flatly deny the word of God. *"You surely shall not die!"* he affirms. Then with slander that Eve should have detected as being false, he says in effect, "God has been holding out on you. He doesn't want you to enjoy the best in life. *For God knows that in the day you eat of the tree your eyes will be opened, and you will be like Him, knowing good and evil."*

Satan's approach has been most clever. He has implied that restrictions are evil. God's plan contains restrictions. His plan, therefore, must be evil. In three short sentences he has questioned the goodness of God, denied the severity of God, and slandered the motive of God.

And Eve has been swept along by his reasoning.

In Satan's approach to Eve we see clearly his strategy. His words and his deeds are evident. There are only three avenues of approach which the devil can use to tempt us. These are described by the apostle John: *"For everything in the world— the lust of the flesh* [what I want to do], *the lust of the eyes* [what I want to have], *and the pride of life* [what I want to be]—*comes not from the Father but from the world* (1 John 2:16).

All of us possess the innate desire to enjoy things and satisfy the human appetites which God has given us. Sin enters the picture when we gratify these desires beyond the bounds set by God. This is the lust of the flesh. We also like to obtain things, but if we become greedy and hoard possessions for their own sake, we go beyond the parameters of the ordinate and are consumed by our inordinate desires. When this happens we fall prey to the lust of the eyes. And then there is the natural desire to act independently of God and so achieve our own purpose. When our ambitious plans leave God out and are achieved at the expense of others, or by unscrupulous means, and when our goals become an overriding obsession, then this is evidence of the pride of life.

In the case of Eve, Satan led her to feel that she and Adam were being unjustly deprived of something. The mere hint of this excited her desire for it. He then boldly charged that what God had said was not true but was being used to keep them back from seeking the best. He then offered an inducement and promised *"you shall become like God."* And Eve looked at the fruit and saw that it was good for food (the lust of the flesh), and that it was a delight to the eye (the lust of the eyes), and desirable to make one wise (the pride of life), and she took of the tree. She yielded in every point from which temptation could come.

WHEN WEDDING FRILLS WEAR OFF

But why did Eve do this? What caused her to act independently of her husband? Hadn't God made them "joint proprietors" of the Garden?

It seems as if Adam and Eve, in spite of all the blessings they enjoyed, had begun to drift apart.[5] The result was that *Eve made a decision without consulting Adam.*

This illustrates the painfully obvious fact that honeymoons do not last forever. The pressure of daily affairs occupy our minds, and unless there is a determined effort on our part to share our ideals and aspirations, we begin slowly to drift apart. The danger facing each one of us is that the drift may become a rift.

In marriage today a man and his wife must find time, however briefly, to communicate as persons. They must realize that only to the degree that they reflectively treat each other's wishes with respect, discuss their goals, evaluate their system of values, and analyze their deepest longings, can they enjoy proper communication.

Marriage may be likened to a fabric which must be woven together from spiritual threads. The possibility of the intrusion of worldly standards is ever present. That is why the apostle John began his warning by saying *"Do not love the world or anything that is in the world. If anyone loves the world, the love of the Father is not in him"* (1 John 2:15).

The first thing a couple should do to guard against drifting apart is pray together. So often all the other experiences of life are shared—talking, loving, and crying—but only prayer and communion with God can lead them to a deeper level in their human relationship. This should be followed by regular Bible study and fellowship with other Christian couples. The problem with Eve was that she lost sight of the spiritual dimension, acted independently, and took of the fruit without discussing matters with her husband.

END OF AN ERA

By the time Adam comes looking for his wife, she has prepared their meal. She eats of the fruit and also gives some of it to Adam. Eve expects to become like God. Instead of having her expectations fulfilled, she feels a strange and uneasy sensation come over her body. It is something she has not experienced before. She feels naked.[6]

Adam, knowing full well what his wife has done, deliberately eats some of the fruit (1 Tim. 2:14). His sin is willful. He then experiences the same feeling of nakedness. Instinctively he and Eve make aprons of leaves. Instead of being like God, they feel the cutting edge of guilt, and when God comes to commune with them they hide from Him. Sin has destroyed their fellowship.

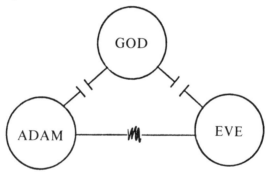

The image of God which they share is now marred. Their intellect becomes darkened, their emotions are degraded, and their will is deadened. They can no longer relate to God as before. Sin has separated them from Him. In time they will find that it will also mar their relationship with each other.

As a result of the entrance of sin into the world God condemns the serpent to crawl on his belly (Gen. 3:14). Satan is set at enmity with the seed of the woman (v. 15), and his doom is predicted. Eve and all women are assigned pain in childbirth and are required to submit to their husbands (v. 16); and Adam, who had sinned willfully, is sentenced to lifelong toil and hardship (vv. 17-19).

God graciously makes clothing for Adam and Eve. This necessitates the death of animals, and it is highly probable that at this time He instructs them in the mode of sacrifices. God then expels Adam and Eve from the Garden *"lest they should eat of the tree of life and live forever."* If they had eaten of the fruit of this tree they would have possessed eternal life, but with all the limitations of their fallen, depraved, human bodies and personalities. God, however, promises Eve an heir—a promise which ultimately would be fulfilled in the Lord Jesus Christ—and, by keeping the way to the tree of life open, provides Adam and Eve and their descendants with the promise of hope and of eternal life.[7]

EYE OF THE BEHOLDER

One thing which modern women find most displeasing in this account is the fact that from this time onwards Eve is told that Adam will rule over her (Gen. 3:16; see Eph. 5:22; Col. 3:18; 1 Pet. 3:1, 5). In yielding to Satan's blandishments she sought for control. As a penalty she is now to be controlled. But does this mean that she is inferior to her husband? What of the equality they formerly shared? How are we to understand Eve's subordination to her husband?

In the fall the divine image which Adam and Eve shared was marred. They were still equal as persons. The fact that Eve was placed under her husband's authority does not mean that she was now inferior. It merely means that in their new environment, having been thrust out of the Garden, and having to endure hardship and trial, privation and loss, she needs her husband's protection.

Eve was "conned" by Satan (1 Tim. 2:14). She was deceived. From that time onward the deference a wife is to give her husband is in recognition of the responsibility laid upon *him* by God for her protection.

Those who make a great issue over a wife's subjection to her husband overlook the fact that all of us are subject to someone. We are all subject to the President of the United States and to those officials who act as the appointed representatives of the constituted government of this country. Employees are subject to their employers. Even directors of large corporations are responsible to the board. There is no escaping the fact that all of us, regardless of our sex, are subject to a vast number of people. This does not make us inferior to them. We share equality as persons. For the sake of administration, however, there must be proper headship and proper subordination.

This kind of relationship exists even within the Godhead. We know that three eternal co-equal persons make up this Godhead. These are God the Father, God the Son, and God the Holy Spirit. Within the Godhead, however, there is willing subordination. We read in the Scriptures that, for the purpose of carrying out the divine decree, Christ the Son submitted himself to the authority of the Father (Heb. 2:7-9). Even in the eternal state He will exercise leadership *under* the headship of the Father (1 Cor. 15:24, 28). The same may be said for the Holy Spirit. He was sent forth into the world by the Father and the Son (John 15:26; 16:7). He is not inferior to the other two members of the Godhead. However, for the purpose of carrying out the will of the Godhead, He has assumed a role subordinate to the Father and the Son.

The greatest fear a woman has is that if she submits to her husband's authority he may take advantage of her. Of course it is easy for a husband to become irritated by his wife's foibles, or take her for granted. That is why Paul found it necessary to remind men to show their wives the same self-sacrificing love that Christ shows for the Church (Eph. 5:22). And Peter counseled those in his day to be considerate of their wives and treat them with respect as joint heirs of the grace of life so that nothing would hinder their prayers (1 Pet. 3:7; note vv. 1-6). Where true love is present, the wife will not feel that she is a "glorified housemaid" or a "sex object." She will be able to respond in a positive way to her husband's loving concern for her well-being. She will then learn that nothing can produce unity in the home better than the democratic process of consultation, discussion, and the free exchange of ideas. Unfortunately for Eve, she overlooked this important point.

All of this does not mean that a wife cannot work, write, or follow a career. She can. In her relationship to her husband, however, she should continue to be supportive (1 Tim. 2:13).

To maintain the divine order, submission to headship is not only desirable but necessary (1 Cor. 11:3). And within such headship the husband is to show his wife the same kind of love the Lord Jesus shows His Church!

Interaction

1. Discuss Satan's timing in the temptation of Eve. How did she feel about (a) God, and (b) her husband? Why was she so vulnerable? What does this teach us about the way in which we are tempted?
2. In 2 Corinthians 2:11 the apostle Paul stated that we are ignorant of Satan's devices. How does 1 John 2:15-16 and the temptation of Eve shed light on Paul's statement? In what ways may we be aware of the strategies he uses?
3. Progress from temptation to sin was described by James (1:13-15). In what specific ways does Eve illustrate this progression? What should she have done to avoid Satan's trap? Why are we so apt to blame others when the consequences of our misdeeds catch up with us?
4. When sin entered the world, fellowship with God was broken. How may this be restored? What provision has God made for our restoration to the image in which Adam and Eve were created (Rom. 8:29; 1 Cor. 15:49; 2 Cor. 3:18; Eph. 1:18-20, 22-23; Col. 3:10, 12-17)? How may this be achieved?
5. Submission is a hard lesson for us to learn. Why? Why has it become the "battleground" for the "war between the sexes"? What example does God set for us? Probe the ways in which living as God requires—in the home, church, and society—brings glory to Him and peace to ourselves (1 Cor. 16:16; Col. 3:18-20; Heb. 13:17; Jas. 4:7; 1 Pet. 2:13; 3:1-7; 5:5).

3

WORM IN THE APPLE

Let every Christian father and mother understand, when the child is three years old, that they have done more than half of all they will ever do for his character.
—Horace Bushnell

Genesis 4

It was summer time. Each afternoon, with monotonous regularity, the mercury climbed into the upper 90s. Betty was glad when her sons, Greg, seven, and Scott, five, would play outside in the mornings, for then she could attend to her work indoors.

On this particular morning, Betty was working in the kitchen. The next thing she knew, a fight was in progress. Running out of the kitchen she saw Greg sitting on top of Scott, pounding him in the face.

It took only a few moments for Betty to reach her sons. She grabbed Greg by the shoulders and pulled him off his brother. Then she demanded, "What's all this about?"

"It's his fault!" Greg charged.

"T'aint!" responded the youngest member of the family bravely, now that his mother was securely positioned between him and his brother.

Then ensued one of those scenes in which a parent will try vainly to probe the issues of a problem only to become frustrated in the process. Fortunately, arguments among children are soon forgotten and harmony can fairly easily be restored.

Not so easily settled are those disputes which continue into adulthood. *Time* magazine recently carried the tragic story of two brothers who were as opposite in temperament as they were similar in appearance.[1] One weekend they met in a cafe. They started quarreling. Later, out in the street, the one brother tried to hitch a ride out of town. When his younger brother saw him he experienced a sudden onrush of pity.

"Come and spend the night in my room," he urged.

His kindness was rudely rejected. Verbal abuse followed, and he and his brother soon came to blows. There was no one to part them, and one of them struck the other and killed him.

An act of sudden passion or the culmination of years of tension? Both. But the provocation in no way excuses the act.

SHOUT OF JOY

It has been said that "the greatest influence on a child begins with the birth of his parents."[2] In the case of Cain and Abel we may be sure that Adam and Eve did all in their power to direct their sons in the way of the Lord. When they were expelled from the Garden, they began to learn firsthand the bitter effect of sin in their own lives and on creation. Whereas Genesis 3 recounts sin's origin, chapter 4 records its progress. In this chapter we pass from a consideration of the individuals involved to the beginning of the family.

"And Adam knew[3] his wife Eve, and she conceived and gave birth to Cain [Qayin] *and said, 'I have acquired* [qana] *a man with* [the help of] *the LORD.' "* This statement, so simple and so natural, has given rise to the misleading theory that Adam and Eve did not have sexual relations with one another while in the Garden of Eden. This would be totally foreign to the purpose of God. He made man and woman sexual beings, and pronounced His work "very good" (Gen. 1:31). If the first act of sexual intimacy was post-Fall, then sex can too easily be identified with our sinful natures and be limited to procreation—a view which is contradicted elsewhere in Scripture (1 Cor. 7:3-5).

The fact that Adam and Eve enjoyed normal sexual relations after the Fall is most important. It shows that they did not harbor resentment towards one another for their expulsion from the Garden. Sex is an expression of love. It is true that a man may engage in sexual intimacy for pleasure without loving his partner; but not so a woman. She wants to feel loved and wanted. In the case of Adam and Eve, their union, stated as emphatically and prominently as it is in the text (Gen. 4:1), indicates the true expression of their love for each other.

True love-making involves both giving and receiving. One of the most frustrating experiences in the life of either a man or a woman is when one tries to initiate love-making and the other is too tired, or, for one reason or another, is apathetic and unresponsive. This might easily have been Eve's experience (note the close connection between Gen. 3:17-19 and 4:1. Gen. 3:20-24 may be regarded as parenthetic). It would have been natural for Adam to come home from the fields worn out with the day's exertions. For them to achieve proper harmony, Adam would have had to keep Eve's needs in mind and properly order his responsibilities; and Eve must have displayed the same "mystique" she did before the Fall. Such mutual consideration forms the basis of a healthy relationship.

In the course of time Eve conceives and bears a son whom she names Cain ("acquired"). It seems as if she believed that her son would be the deliverer whom God had promised (Gen. 3:15). "Though Eve was mistaken in her hope," observes Martin Luther, "her words show that she was a pious woman who believed the promise of the coming salvation through the blessed Savior."

How long a time elapsed between the birth of Eve's first and second sons we have no means of knowing. There is, however, evidence of her growing disillusionment with life for her second son is given the name "Abel" meaning "vapor, vanity." Apparently what the Psalmist later spoke of as being the universal experience of parents (Ps. 58:3) was proving to be true for both her and her husband. In all probability Adam and Eve had begun to learn that *"foolishness is bound up in the heart of a child"* (Prov. 22:15a) and that *"a foolish son is a grief to his father and a bitterness to her who bore him"* (Prov. 17:25; 29:15b).

We should not be too severe in our censure of Adam and Eve for the way Cain turned out. They were the first parents and had no previous example to follow. They were also acutely aware of their own failure and may, therefore, have been more inclined to excuse their son's shortcomings when they saw the fruit of their misdeeds appearing in him. By comparison, we are in a most enviable position. We have

God's Word to guide us and can rear our children in the nurture and admonition of the Lord.[4]

CONFLICT OVER ACCEPTANCE

But imagine being Abel and carrying through life a name testifying to the disillusionment of your parents. Perhaps this is what drove him to a life of faith (Heb. 11:4). In all probability (as with many young people since his time) he felt the need of acceptance and reached out to God for the peace and security he needed.

In pursuing the narrative, we find that the sons of Adam and Eve follow different vocations. Cain cultivates crops and Abel raises livestock.[5] And *"in the course of time* [when they are grown men] *Cain brings an offering to the LORD of the fruit of the ground. Abel also brings* [an offering] *of the firstlings of his flock . . . And the LORD has regard for Abel and his offering; but for Cain and for his offering He has no regard."*

But why did God reject Cain's offering?[6]

The most common explanation given by evangelical commentators that Cain's offering was bloodless and that God had demonstrated the need for atonement (and the covering of sin) when he slew animals in Eden and made clothes for Adam and Eve (Gen. 2:21). The Old Testament, however, teaches that God will reject the most perfect sacrifice if the heart of the offerer is not right before Him (comp. Isa. 1:11-13; Hos. 6:6; Micah 6:6-8). Furthermore, the word translated "offering" is *minchah* (not *'olah,* the usual term for a blood offering) and is used in the Levitical laws for a bloodless thank offering (Lev. 2:1, 4, 14, 15). The value of the offering is therefore seen to depend upon the character and disposition of the offerer.

When Cain's offering is rejected he becomes very angry. He displays his feelings of hostility, and his countenance falls.[7]

FAMILIAR STEREOTYPES

There are three basic causes of anger (hostility). The first is *rejection* by an emotionally significant individual or group. When this happens we suffer the pangs of insecurity and lose our sense of belonging. The second basic cause of anger is *frustration.* We feel frustrated when events do not work out as we had planned. When this happens, we become angry because we are no longer in control. The third basic cause of anger is *humiliation.* We want to be admired, looked up to, respected, and praised by others. This contributes to our feeling of worth. However, when we are belittled, we suffer from a lowered sense of esteem.

It is very difficult for us to live with rejection. When we feel rejected a destructive cycle begins. Our emotional response to rejection is to feel worthless and this is followed by the sensation of self-hate. But self-hate is too painful for us and so we develop an escape mechanism. This device may take several forms, such as bullying or bragging, repetitious illnesses, drugs or alcohol, deviant sexual behavior, projecting our hate onto someone else, developing a pseudo-pleasing character in an attempt to win the acceptance of others, or even religious "fanaticism." Unfortunately for us, these devices lead to further rejection (e.g., "nobody likes a bully, an alcoholic, a pervert," etc.), and this results in increased feelings of worthlessness, self-hate, etc.

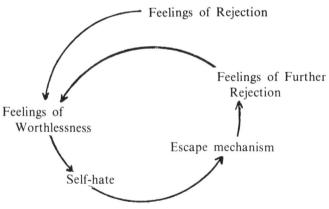

THE CYCLE OF REJECTION

In Cain's experience he feels rejected when God refuses to accept his offering. His countenance falls (i.e., he feels worthless and suffers from loss of a sense of esteem). God asks him about his feelings and promises, *"If you do well, will not your countenance be lifted up?"* God is showing Cain how to break the "rejection syndrome." He is also warning him of the consequences of destructive self-will (i.e., self-hate). *"If you do not do well, sin is crouching* [as a beast] *at the door; and its desire is for you, but you must master it."*

Unfortunately for Cain, he does not respond positively to God's invitation, nor does he heed His counsel. On the one hand he refuses to acknowledge his sin, and on the other finds that he cannot live with his self-hate. He therefore projects his anger onto someone else—Abel. In this connection the Hebrew text is most revealing. It reads: *"And Cain said to Abel his brother, ————."* Apparently his anger is so intense that he becomes incoherent. And in his rage he rises up against Abel and kills him.

HOTLINE DISSENT

But the cycle of rejection does not end with the death of Abel. Inner misgivings, feelings of guilt, the fact that "no one likes a murderer," leads to further feelings of worthlessness. And the cycle continues so that when God approaches Cain again, Cain responds with arrogant hostility.

It is significant that God again seeks the sinner. He comes looking for Cain, and asks: *"Where is Abel your brother?"* Cain's response is most revealing. Unwilling to admit his culpability, he projects his anger on God. *"I don't know,"* is his retort. *"Am I my brother's keeper?"* You are wrong to even question about him. His arrogance is mingled with sarcasm and a complete disregard of the One to whom he is speaking.

But this attempt to shrug off his feelings of guilt is no way to handle the problem. God knows only too well what Cain has done. Civil government has not yet been instituted and so the murderer's life will not be forfeited (see Gen. 9:5-6). However, Cain is to be punished (Gen. 4:11-15); and loneliness, hardship, and fear will be a daily part of his experience.

When sentence is pronounced on Cain, he *"goes out from the presence of the LORD and settles in the land of Nod, east of Eden."* There he builds a city and starts a civilization which is characterized by the same rejection of God. There is no recognition of the exceeding sinfulness of sin or thought of salvation. Instead, Cain's descendants glory in their wickedness and feel that they can sin with impunity (comp. Gen. 4:23-24).

FILLING IN THE BLANKS

Two problems remain: Why was Cain afraid that someone might kill him? and, Where did he obtain his wife?

The answer to these problems is connected. It is not necessary to postulate a pre-Adamic race before God made Adam and Eve. From Genesis 1:28 we know that Adam and Eve were to be fruitful and multiply and fill the earth. From Genesis 4:25 and 5:3-4 we know that they had other sons and daughters. Considering the longevity of those who lived before the flood, the human race would have multiplied quite rapidly.[8] Of whom, then, was Cain afraid? The answer seems to be that he feared retaliation from his own brothers and sisters (or perhaps even from his parents).

And where did he find a woman to marry? In all probability one of his sisters idolized him (as sisters will sometimes do) and chose to leave home with him. While this seems strange to us because of our cultural conditioning, it was really quite logical that at this early stage in the development of the human race a man would marry his sister. Seeing the human race developed from a single pair, the marriage of brother and sister was, for a time, a necessity.

BREAKING THE CYCLE

The murder of Abel and the departure of Cain must have caused Adam and Eve considerable grief. It must also have been a source of concern to them that their first-born son had repudiated the worship of the Lord and had become a man of violence. In this respect they share the problem of many modern parents. Many of us become frustrated over the rearing of our children. We are intimidated by the rapid changes that have taken place and the speed with which our children become independent. We are fearful of worldly influences and try to protect our sons and daughters from them, even to the extent of sending them to Christian schools and colleges. In spite of these efforts, it seems as if we grow farther and farther apart.

What then can be done to aid us, and them, in this dilemma? How may we rear our children so as to counteract the trend towards violence?

The late Hubert Humphrey, while serving as Vice President under Lyndon Johnson, gave his assessment of the situation. "This country is in trouble . . ." he said. "The violence we have witnessed, however inexcusable, is only a symptom of a much deeper problem—a problem of poverty and hopelessness." Unfortunately, the statesman from Minnesota omitted from his remarks all thought of spiritual realities—sin and one's alienation from God—and the influence of godly parents. Winston Churchill was, therefore, much closer to the truth when he stated: "There is no doubt that it is around the family and the home that all the greatest virtues, the most dominating virtues of human society, are created, strengthened, and maintained."

But how may we cultivate these virtues? To be sure, it is in the home that life's first and most basic lessons are learned. From the home, in the attitude of the parents, comes the beginnings of attitudes and ideals that later on will dominate the adult life of our children. And so in considering how we may best rear our children we must, of necessity, begin with ourselves.

While it may sound trite to emphasize the need for a genuine commitment to spiritual values, only by practicing such a commitment can we hope to rear happy, healthy, well-adjusted children.

Modern man—in other words, all of us!—struggles with feelings of insecurity. These feelings are increased by our susceptibility to *rejection, humiliation,* and *frustration.*[9] The antidote to rejection is a sense of *belonging.* The remedy for humiliation is found in a realization of our *worth.* And the answer to frustration is *competence.*

This is how it works. Through a personal appreciation of what the Bible teaches us about God the Father, we come to know experientially our acceptance by Him. When we learn of His love for us and the provision He has made for our salvation, we rejoice in our standing as His children. We are united to Him by ties which nothing can sever. We belong to Him and this sense of *belonging* can become a dynamic reality in our lives. It is the only power strong enough to counteract the hostility (anger) which rejection engenders.

Second, as we consider all that God the Son accomplished for us on the cross, we come to appreciate our *worth*. Not only did He die for our redemption but those who put their trust in Him become joint-heirs with Him of all the glories of the Father's Kingdom. As we read through the New Testament and apply these precious truths to our lives, we will gladly submit to His right to rule in our lives. This sense of worth, based on the forgiveness offered us in Christ, is the only adequate remedy for our feelings of guilt.

Third, by means of the indwelling ministry of God the Holy Spirit, we are made equal to every task. In a word, He makes us *competent*. This does not mean that we suddenly and miraculously succeed at everything we attempt. It does mean that He empowers us for service. We can even face adversity for, under His sovereign control, we are able to handle all the things which otherwise might upset our emotional equilibrium. His empowering provides an adequate corrective to fear and frustration which otherwise might incapacitate us and neutralize our natural gifts.

Now, with inner security a blessed reality in our lives, we can turn our attention to the rearing of our children. From their earliest years we can instill in them the need for dedication to the Lord and submission to His authority. We can instruct them in the importance of Bible study, and by developing a strong personal identity (through a vital relationship with each member of the Trinity), they can then grow up strong in the faith. In other words, a strong parent can develop a strong child.

But what of the rejection syndrome?

When others reject us (or our children), we (or they) will be able to break the cycle by realizing that God is far more significant than anyone else. By strengthening our relationship with Him, we will be able to rise above the crises which otherwise might engulf us. This is what God offered Cain— the possibility of personal wholeness. And these same provisions He makes available to us.

Interaction

1. Discuss the following: "The circumstances of your life, good or bad, are important, but not decisive. *You* are decisive. When you fail it is not your parents' fault. They may have failed you at some crucial point in time, but your actions (or reactions) now are your responsibility."

2. Probe the manner in which God dealt with Cain. Why did He ask questions? What kinds of questions did He ask? How might a positive response on Cain's part have led to a resolution to his problem? When did God leave off speaking with Cain? What may Christian parents learn from their heavenly Father's example?

3. *Good character* (though an old-fashioned phrase) is what parents still desire for their children. It implies honesty, tolerance, and confidence in oneself and respect for others. These virtues cannot be developed without training, demonstration (i.e., example) and encouragement. In what practical ways may parents develop these traits in their children?

4. What contributes to violence? Where does violence originate? According to one report, serious, violent crimes are increasing nine times faster than the rate of birth. What responsibility does this place on Christian parents? How may they successfully counteract the influence of the world in the lives of their children?

5. Why may a Christian enjoy better mental health than a non-Christian? What does salvation provide that counteracts the debilitating effects of hostility, guilt, or fear? How does this contribute to one's emotional well-being?

4

TRAIN UP A CHILD

It seems no matter how you encourage your children to tred in the paths of righteousness, they insist in following in your footsteps.

—Arnold Glasow

Genesis 5:21-24

Some years ago Dick, a young man in his early 20s, met Sue, an attractive young girl in her late teens. They began dating and twelve months later were married. Dick's parents had been divorced when he was seven, and he had grown to manhood without the guiding influence of a father. Now, as a husband, he did not know how to show his wife the love he felt for her.

Two years after their marriage, Sue presented Dick with a son. In his new role as a father, he had no model to follow. He did not know how to relate to the boy who soon would be looking to him for guidance and direction.

Dick's situation is by no means unique. In the home children learn from their parents. A young boy learns from his father how to be a man and how to show proper love, care, and respect to his mother. From his mother he learns what women are like and how they are to be treated. In time, what he has acquired from his parents he will transfer to the person who becomes his wife.

Likewise a young girl learns from her mother how to be a woman and cultivate those virtues which will make her a good wife and mother. And from her father she learns what men are like and how she may be supportive of them.

One's parents, therefore, are the single most important influence in the life of a child. They rear their child by their example. The home they establish should provide a climate conducive to the moral and spiritual, intellectual and physical development of those who will become a part of the family circle. Only by means of a strong home can we develop a strong child and counteract the secular, materialistic, and irreligious values of our modern society.

But how are parents to build strong homes?

Realizing the problems facing each one of us, it is refreshing to turn to the example of Enoch for encouragement and guidance. He faced the same kinds of tensions we face, and in many respects becomes a prototype which provides us with a solution to our problems. As we examine the Scripture record, we find that it is not sufficient for us to give our children comfortable and convenient homes in which to live, or books, toys, sports equipment, and clothing. We must give of ourselves in constructive ways. As we do so, our children will learn to give of themselves, and the happiness they derive from this will, in turn, establish their values and regulate their lives.

OPPOSING VALUES

Following Adam and Eve's expulsion from the garden and the murder of Abel, two separate traditions begin to develop. These are headed by Cain and Seth. Cain and his descendants are godless, whereas those of the line of Seth retain some semblance of godliness.

In the days following the establishment of Cain's city, civilization thrives. The arts (Gen. 4:21) and sciences (Gen. 4:17b, 22) flourish. But the flowering of these cultural values is not sufficient to hold in check the evils of man's fallen nature, and the circumstances and conditions of men deteriorate. Lamech, a descendant of Cain and a contemporary of Enoch, is the first to institute polygamy. In doing so he sets in motion a course of action which leads to the abandonment of principles and the degeneration of the race. Furthermore, the way in which he boasts of a murder of a young man shows the violence and lawlessness of the age.

Something of the irreligious character of the conditions surrounding Enoch may be gleaned from two important facts. First, it is at this time that those of the godly line of

Seth begin to call on the Lord in prayer (Gen. 4:26b). Second, when Enoch begins to walk with the Lord, the Hebrew text places the emphasis on "*the* God." This is at once qualitative and comparative. It points to the genuineness of Enoch's experience and, at the same time, contrasts the reality of his encounter with the religious observances of those about him. Whatever form of worship they follow, it is a substitute for genuine fellowship with God.

Further confirmation of the irreligious character of Enoch's contemporaries may be culled from other portions of Scripture. The Psalmist touches on their flagrant rejection of God's grace when he quotes them as saying, *"God has forgotten, He hides His face* [from our sin]. *He will never see it . . ."* (Ps. 10:11), and *"How does God know* [of our sin]? *Is there knowledge with the most High?"* (Ps. 73:11). Even Eliphaz refers to the blasphemy of these men. He says to Job, *"Will you keep the old way which wicked men have trodden, who were snatched away before their time, whose foundation was poured out as a stream, who said to God, 'Depart from us;' and 'What can the Almighty do for*[1] *them* (i.e., the godly)?' "* (Job 22:15-17).

The men of Enoch's time felt that they could sin with impunity. They thought that God would not see them, and that even if He could, He would not take notice of what they were doing. In this respect they were much like people today. The prevailing attitude in our society seems to be that we can break God's law, flaunt His standards, and get away with it.

PATTERN AND PROCESS

For the first sixty-five years of his life, Enoch lives the same kind of life as the other descendants of Seth. He is outwardly godly, but subject to the same encroachments of evil and the slow deterioration of his moral values. Then a baby boy is born into his home. *"And Enoch walks with God after he begets Methuselah"* (Gen. 5:22). As Enoch holds his son in his arms and feels the tiny fingers run over his face and grasp his hair, he wants the best for his son. He begins to imagine how his son will grow up, the kind of profession he will follow, and the way in which he will take his place in the community. He has great ambitions for Methuselah and he is determined to do everything possible to help him achieve them.

Then, with a sense of fear, Enoch suddenly realizes that his son will grow to manhood in a dreadful and terrible world. How will he cope with the unbridled pride and flagrant lawlessness of the Cainites? The thought is frightening. What can he do to protect Methuselah from such a wicked environment? Should he drop out of society and go off into the hills with his family and start a new community? Should he rear his son as an introverted mystic?

In groping for answers Enoch finally realizes that the best thing he can do is to set his son a good example. He can show his son that if he is to live in this world and remain free from its contaminating influences he will have to be a man of principles. And from this moment Enoch orders his life so that his son will have an example to follow.[2]

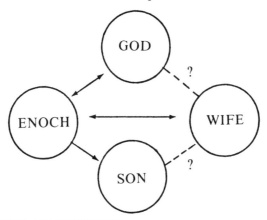

CREATIVE PRECEDENT

As parents we have the privilege of rearing our children during their most impressionable years. Many of the fundamental attitudes they develop, and the way in which they will later respond to external stimuli, are formulated during this early period of growth. If, in our homes, we do not develop proper values and lay a foundation for the cultivation of healthy relationships for our children, then no organization will be able to make up for our failure and their loss.

Enoch's influence on his son is positive. While the wickedness and lawlessness remain, he sets Methuselah an example. His example includes both counsel and direction. He counsels him on what to avoid and directs his footsteps in the way he should go (see Prov. 22:6). He knows that in and of himself he is insufficient for the task of rearing his son. He therefore walks with God, and as he does so he is able to show Methuselah how he himself should live.

Enoch also denounces the errors of the time and warns the godless people that the Lord will judge them for their ungodly deeds (Jude 1:14-15). This kind of "negative" teaching is shunned today. Psychologists tell us that prohibitions will set limits on the development of our children and dwarf their growth. Unfortunately, they interpret biblical principles as a set of rules and accuse Christians who live "according to the Book" of being legalistic (comp. Matt. 11:29-30; John 8:32). They forget that the God of all wisdom gave definite counsel to the sons of Israel on what they should and should not do (Exod. 20—23). Even the Lord Jesus did not hesitate to warn His disciples of the hypocrisy of the Pharisees and the contaminating influence of Herod (Matt. 16:6; Mark 8:5).

In rearing our children, we need to remember that the bricks of character are laid one by one. Each parent must have his "plumbline" (i.e., his principles) by which to measure right from wrong. In the building of character, the "plumbline" is of the utmost importance, for if the walls are crooked, the doors and windows will not fit correctly and the roof may tumble in. In the end, the "house" is fit only to be torn down or abandoned.

As Christian parents we may learn from Enoch. It is our solemn responsibility to set an example of godliness for our children. We need to nurture them in the principles of righteousness and truthfulness, an appreciation of the dignity of work and the need for devotion to duty, faithfulness to the Lord and adherence to sound doctrine, respect for others and loyalty to their country. The character thus developed will not be the product of a set of rules but the result of a system of values which has been observed to be superior.

A task such as this may seem impossible, particularly in the days in which we are living. Enoch realized his insufficiency and drew on the Lord for His sufficiency. He began practicing the principles of righteousness in his own life and this made it easy for Methuselah to follow in his footsteps.

As Enoch walked with God he found that it was not necessary for him to flee from his environment. He could triumph over it. He could also fulfill his responsibilities in all areas of life. He and his wife enjoyed a natural, loving relationship. His leadership in the home—stemming from his walk with the Lord—made it easy for her to respond to him. Other children were born to them; and Enoch set them the same kind of consistent example. And who can tell of the influence Enoch had on the other members of the line of Seth?

True worship always involves self-denial. It is always easier to follow the dictates of the senses rather than the discipline of the Spirit. This fundamental fact has the support of those who have studied the rise and development of religious beliefs from the earliest times to the present. The close kinship between human emotions and the objects worshipped is undeniable. Mankind has invariably made objects of worship that represent his own thoughts and desires (Rom. 1:18-23). The polytheism of the ancient world became very superstitious. Everything was explained in terms of good and evil spirits. And, as the apostle Paul pointed out, in departing from God *people suppressed the truth.* They preferred their wickedness to the knowledge of the Lord. God, therefore, gave them over in the sinful desires of their hearts to sexual impurity for the degrading of their bodies with one another. Even as they did not see fit to acknowledge God any longer, He gave them over to a reprobate mind, to become filled with all sorts of unrighteousness, wickedness, greed, and malice so that not only were their lives characterized by all kinds of evil, but they did not hesitate to give their hearty approval to those who practiced the same vices (Rom. 1:24-32).

It was in such an environment that Enoch walked with *"the God."*

THE GOAL OF LIFE

Conditions are no worse today than they were in Enoch's time. We are surrounded by immoral living and the perversion of justice. Lust, hatred, and violence are brought before us daily. How then are we to live consistent lives before our children?

As Enoch walked with the Lord, He gave him a promise which was designed to encourage him when the going was rough. God knew that Enoch would need strengthening when the vicissitudes of life pressed in upon him. God gave him an expectation which would motivate him to persevere even when his children were grown. God told him that he would be translated. And Enoch believed God's promise. In Hebrews 11:5 we read, *"By faith Enoch was translated. . . ."* He had no precedent to rely on, for no one had ever been translated before. Everyone he had ever known had died. Faith in this promise stimulated him to walk consistently. It motivated him to maintain close fellowship with the One who had made this promise to him. He knew that at any moment God might bring about its fulfillment.

A similar promise has been made to all believers. The apostle Paul tells us about it in 1 Corinthians 15. *"Behold, I show you a mystery.*[3] *We shall not all sleep* [die] *but we shall be changed in a moment, in the twinkling of an eye, at the last trumpet. For the trumpet shall sound, and the dead will be raised imperishable, and* we shall be changed" (1 Cor. 15:51-52). Earlier in his life when Paul wrote his first letter to the Thessalonian Christians, he emphasized the same expectation. *"For this we declare to you by the word of the Lord, that we who are alive, who are left until the coming of the Lord, shall not precede those who have fallen asleep, for the Lord Himself shall descend from heaven with a cry of command, with the archangel, call, and with the sound of the trumpet of God. And the dead in Christ will rise first;* then we who are alive, who are left, shall be caught up together with Him in the clouds to meet the Lord in the air; and so shall we ever be with the Lord" (1 Thess. 4:13-17).

We do not know when He will return, but we have His promise that He will do so. It may be while we are sitting at our desks at the office or working in the factory. It may be while we are bending over the kitchen sink or cleaning the house. It may be as we are riding the subway or the bus. It may be during a time of recreation with our children or at church. At any moment we may be caught up into the presence of the Lord. With this expectation before us, what kind of people should we be? The apostle John answers this question. He tells us that *"everyone who has this hope in him purifies himself"* (1 John 3:3). The reality of this hope should infuse us with new life. It should give us new goals, a new purpose, new motives, and change our system of values.

From the guidelines in Genesis 5, we find that whenever a husband and father is realistic about himself, knows his strengths and weaknesses, and is prepared to follow God's will, he will develop a balanced perspective on life. His own abilities will improve. He will begin to exercise the proper leadership within the family circle and this will result in healthy interpersonal relationships. When he demonstrates his selfless love for his wife he can expect her to respond to his leadership (Eph. 5:25-29).

While the text does not say so, the thought left in our minds is that Enoch and his wife enjoyed warm companionship. Other children were born into their home and this in itself involves the maturing of their love and the growth of their personalities. Whether Enoch's wife was spiritually compatible or not, we do not know. There exists the strong possibility that, from a spiritual point of view, Enoch had no human with whom he might enjoy in-depth fellowship. If this was indeed the case, then his experience was not unique. One of the greatest problems facing couples today is in the area of their spiritual development. They should work towards compatibility and spiritual harmony.

By demonstrating his selfless love for his wife, a husband can secure a positive response which will create a suitable climate in the home for the rearing of their children. From his example, his sons will learn proper love and respect for their mother. His daughters will see in him the kind of man they hope one day to marry. And if these principles are learned early enough from a consistent example, then they, as young people, will be less inclined to go rushing off into unwise marriages, and their parents will spend less time worrying about the kind of person their son or daughter is dating.

But where does all this begin?

In the consistent, godly example of a husband and father.

Interaction

1. Consider your own parents. List three positive ways in which their lives made an impact on yours. Share with one another how you were influenced by (a) your father, and (b) your mother.* [If you were not reared by your parents, substitute those who did rear you, or two people who have greatly influenced you for (a) and (b) above.]

2. What parallels can you draw between the society established by Cain and our society today. What influence does the environment of your children (friends, school, neighborhood) have on their *total* development? How are you counteracting any evil influences?

3. Do you think that Enoch's wife was spiritually as sensitive or matured the way he did? Why? What does this teach us about our relationships?

4. What can you, as a Christian parent, learn from Enoch? How do you plan to work out in your life and experience what you have learned?

5. Of what value is a knowledge of future prophetic events? How did God's promise to Enoch influence him? In what ways does a belief in Christ's soon return (a) provide an "anchor" for our hope, (b) give us a sense of security, and (c) act as a purifying agent on our lives?

---

*Further information on the lasting impact of one's parents may be found in *Your Inner Child of the Past* by W. Hugh Missildine (New York: Simon and Schuster, 1963).

5

THE MYTH THAT OPPOSITES ATTRACT

Behind every great man there stands a woman.
—Anonymous

Genesis 6

On hearing a marriage counselor use the above quotation in a special lecture at a mid-western university, one cynical student was overheard to add, ". . . telling him he's wrong."

Ironically, both statements may be true. Depending on the circumstances a wife can be either the greatest asset or the biggest liability in her husband's life. It generally takes a strong woman to marry a strong man. Strong women as a rule do not marry weak men. If they do, the marriage may not last; and if it does, it probably will not be a happy one.

In this connection, had Katherine Von Bora been unequal in her role as the wife of Martin Luther, the great reformer, their marriage might have hindered the Protestant cause. As it turned out, Katherine was both the inspirer and the encourager of her husband. She shared with him the ardors of his life, encouraged him when he was on the verge of despair, and supported him in the midst of all the pressures of his ministry. It is no wonder that Martin Luther wrote: "The greatest gift of God is a pious, amiable spouse who fears God, loves His house, and with whom one can live in perfect harmony."

On the other hand, Mary Vazeille, who became the wife of the celebrated John Wesley, opposed him in public and harangued him in private. She was unsympathetic with his aims and uncooperative with his schedule. She made his life so miserable that when she finally deserted him, he was glad to be rid of her. Unfortunately, she took with her some of his journals and papers which were never returned.

PROVERBS 31:10-11

No one can deny that Noah is one of the great figures of the Old Testament. He is singled out by God as being one of three men of exemplary conduct (Ezek. 14:14, 20), and the writer of the letter to the Hebrews speaks of him as being a person of outstanding faith (Heb. 11:7). But what of his wife? What role did she play in the events which climaxed in the Flood? Was her role supportive or did she make his task all the harder by her criticism or opposition?

While the Bible—owing to the brevity and selectivity of the record—does not mention Mrs. Noah specifically, it does give the impression that she supported her husband in his building of the ark (1 Peter 3:20; 2 Peter 2:5). In fact, the more closely we study the narrative the more clearly we come to see her identification with him in his beliefs. Living positively with unhappy situations—a godless environment, the constant threat of violence, the perversion of justice, and the loss of one's possessions—does not come automatically. In times like these it is all too easy for the unlovely side of one's nature to show through. And any lack of spiritual sensitivity could easily be excused. After all, it was Noah who received the communication from the Lord. Mrs. Noah learned of God's intention through her husband. It would have been easy for her to set aside this strange requirement as a new manifestation of her husband's "religious fanaticism," or attach less weight to God's words than they deserved. Only through close fellowship with her husband in the things of the Lord was she able to share with him the reality of what was to happen. We may therefore conclude that Mrs. Noah was one on whom her husband could rely for support.

MARGINALIA

Several problems face us as we begin our study of Genesis 6—9. First, who were the *"sons of God"*? Were they angelic beings (1 Peter 3:19-20; 2 Peter 2:4-5), or the descendants of the godly line of Seth? Most commentators favor the latter view and Dr. J. Sidlow Baxter has devoted an entire chapter to expounding this theory in his book, *Studies in Problem Texts.*[1]

While the case for equating the *"sons of God"* with the Sethites would seem to be settled, most of those who have written on the subject have worked solely from the English text (comp. Job 1:6; 2:1; 38:7; Dan. 3:25). Some eminent Bible scholars have recently lent their weight to the former view. Among these are Drs. C. Fred Dickason and Merrill F. Unger.[2] In his book, *Biblical Demonology,* Dr. Unger grapples realistically with the problems and offers some constructive ideas. In addition, his discussion of the origin of the *nephilim* (Gen. 6:4; trans. "giants" in the KJV)—who are in many ways a key to the interpretation of the passage—is both instructive and enlightening.

Regardless of which view is preferred, Genesis 6 does give a most important rationale for the Flood (Pss. 10:11; 73:11; Job 22:15-17), and sets the stage for a consideration of the times in which Noah and his family lived.

A second major problem concerns the extent of the Flood. Was it universal or local? Once again the weight of modern opinion favors the latter view. One of the most authoritative writers to advocate a local flood was the late Frederick A. Filby, whose book *The Flood Reconsidered* has been widely received.[3]

The factors supporting a belief in a deluge covering the entire world have been set forth by John C. Whitcomb and Henry M. Morris in *The Genesis Flood.*[4] Furthermore, a consideration of the teaching of the apostle Peter (2 Peter 2:5; 3:5-7) and his use of the Flood in Noah's time as an illustration of God's future judgment by fire (2 Peter 3:10-13) would seem to establish the universality of the Flood beyond question.

While these problems are of considerable interest, we will concentrate our attention on the interpersonal relationships of Noah and his family.

KEEPING THE FAITH

The society of which Noah and his wife are a part (and in which they rear their children) is one of complete disregard for the Lord. As God looks down from heaven He *"sees that the wickedness of man is great . . . and that every intent of*

the thoughts of man's heart is only evil continually." Violence
and corruption prevail (Gen. 6:5, 11).

In contrast to the lawlessness of the times, Noah is found
"blameless."[5] As with Enoch he *"walks with God"*(Gen. 6:9).
God is not "an absent Landlord" where he is concerned, but
rather a vital part of his experience. His relationship with
God touches the very core of his being. It enables him to
establish his life upon the truth.

When a person such as Noah walks with the Lord, we may
be tempted to conclude that his life is therefore free from the
problems that plague the rest of us. Such, however, is not the
case. Noah and his family are compelled to be most selective
in the choice of friends for themselves and playmates for their
children (1 Cor. 15:33). The believers with whom they
fellowship are few, and when it comes time for Noah to
choose suitable wives for his sons, the problem is com-
pounded. The widespread godlessness and corruption make
the selection of God-fearing wives most difficult.

And yet, by walking with the Lord, Noah is able to bring a
strengthening and stabilizing influence to his home. As his
wife responds positively to his leadership, an environment is
created which is conducive to the rearing of their children.
Their spiritual principles safeguard their moral values. In
time, their sons grow to manhood and share the convictions
of their parents. And in all of these matters—the establishing
of their home, the rearing of their children, and finding God-
fearing wives for their sons—the Lord shows Himself to be
sufficient for their needs.

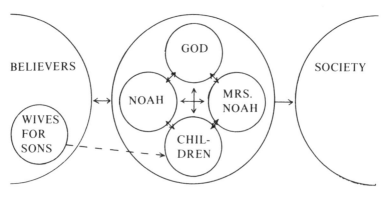

THE PROBLEM OF PERSEVERANCE

God does not promise Noah and his family that they will be translated as was Enoch. Instead, He reveals to him His plan to punish their generation. Nevertheless, one hundred and twenty years of grace will be given them before His judgment falls (Gen. 6:3b, 13). Noah is then told to make an ark. But why make a boat so far from the sea? It's all very well for God to plan to save both Noah and his family, and representatives of all the animals (Gen. 7:2-3), but where is the water to come from? At this period of the earth's history, rain is unknown (Gen. 2:5-6; 7:4).

With the obedience which faith inspires, Noah and his sons begin to build the ark. The task is a difficult one and the work is probably carried on after the routine affairs of earning a living have been taken care of. The building of the ark is a testimony to the people alive at that time and tacitly shows them the fallacy of living only for this world (Heb. 11:10). Noah's contemporaries might live as if this present world was all there was to life (Matt. 24:37-38), but Noah and his family know that the earth is destined to be destroyed. This inspires them to righteousness of life and prevents them from adopting the practices of those about them.

It is also interesting to notice that God only speaks to Noah once (Gen. 6:13-21). This is sufficient. At no time does Noah or any member of his family doubt what God has told them or ask for confirmation of His orders. One hundred and twenty years intervene before God speaks to Noah again; and when He does, it is to command him and his family to enter the ark (Gen. 7:1-4). And Noah obeys. His faith is a living demonstration of his confidence in the One whom he serves. His confidence is based entirely on God's unchanging nature, and he demonstrates the reality of his faith by his prompt obedience.

THE PROBLEM OF (IM)PATIENCE

It is doubtful if anyone really grows towards spiritual maturity without having his or her patience tested (James 1:2-4).

When Noah and his family enter the ark, they face an unforeseen "delay." The door is left open for seven days. This is God's last offer of grace to those living upon the earth. Will they turn from their sinful ways and identify themselves with those whose righteous acts they have ridiculed for so long? At the end of a week of waiting, God closes the door (Gen. 7:16) and soon thereafter convulsive earthquakes shake the land. The *"fountains of the great deep burst open"* and the *"floodgates of the sky are also opened"* (Gen. 7:11). For forty days the rain continues and Noah and his family, who have never experienced anything like this before, witness through the ventilating window a majestic demonstration of God's power in nature. And after the rain ceases, they wait. . . .

At the end of five months the ark comes to rest on the mountains of Ararat (Gen. 8:4) and seventy-four days later the tops of the mountains can be seen. Six weeks more elapse before Noah sends out first a raven and then a dove. Finally, fifty-seven days after Noah has released a dove for the second time, God commands him and his family to leave the ark.

HAPPINESS IS . . .

But what do Noah and his wife and his sons and their wives do during the long months they are cooped up in the ark? Psychologists tell us that any prolonged contact with people—even those whom we love—is detrimental to the relationship. To make matters worse, the home of Noah and his family has been destroyed and the possessions they could not bring into the ark are lost forever. Furthermore, they have no idea where they will be when the ordeal is over. It is relatively easy to maintain a happy atmosphere when all is going well, but to preserve unity in the midst of adverse circumstances is far more demanding. This is where the reality of one's spiritual convictions comes to the fore and prevents a situation from degenerating into an endless round of bickering and complaining.

In the absence of biblical evidence, we can only speculate on how Noah and his family spent the best part of the year.

First, of course, there were the animals to feed and care for. The work load would have to be shared by all eight people. The heavier duties, like toting bales of hay, would undoubtedly have been undertaken by the men, while the women would have gravitated towards nursing any animals that were (sea-) sick and grooming others. The three levels of the ark would also have to be kept livable, and those who have worked on farms will readily understand the tremendous amount of work involved in caring for so many animals as well as the daily grind of having to clean up after them. Since God was a reality to them during the long years they were building the ark, we can presume that He was just as much a reality to them when the Flood covered the ground. They learned from their experience that whatever needed to be done should be done willingly (Eccles. 9:10; Col. 3:17).

In view of the fact that it is a wife and mother who sets the tone of the home, we may be sure it was Mrs. Noah who set about creating a harmonious atmosphere in the ark. And those who have said (and with reason) that you cannot have two women under the same roof, should ponder the prolonged contact of Mrs. Noah and her daughters-in-law. It is also characteristic of men to be the first to chafe under imposed restraints and to want to "go out and do things." When they cannot and tempers become frayed, it is again the women who must "pour oil on troubled waters" and, by their own sweet spirit, take the sting out of a hostile act or a critical remark. Mrs. Noah's threshold of control must have contributed to the harmony of the household and served as an example of godliness-in-action to her daughters-in-law.

And with a proper atmosphere prevailing in the ark, Noah and his family would have had the opportunity to enjoy uninterrupted fellowship with one another. This aspect of family togetherness is missing in many homes today. Outside interests, regular television programs, and even church activities, crowd out the time we should be able to spend with one another. Here again it is often the wife's pervasive influence which takes the structure out of "family togetherness" and makes it a time of rich, rewarding interaction.

THE NEW BEGINNING

The first thing Noah and his family do when they are instructed to leave the ark is to build an altar and offer sacrifices to the Lord (Gen. 8:20-22). They begin by worshipping the One who has so graciously preserved them when all else has been destroyed. Their worship is a fitting commencement of a new period in God's administrative history. He renews his instructions to them by commanding them to *"be fruitful and multiply, and fill the earth"* (Gen. 9:1) and confirms the dominion they are to have over nature. Certain things have changed, however. For the first time they may eat meat (Gen. 9:3). Human government is also committed to them (Gen. 9:6). They are to rule as God's representatives on the earth. Finally, the Lord establishes His covenant with them and promises that, in the future, when rain falls upon the earth, it will never again be in such proportions as to destroy mankind.

Noah now takes his place as the second head of the human race. His three sons, Shem, Ham, and Japheth, become the progenitors of the new tribes (Gen. 10).[6] In many respects they are in an enviable position. Having learned so much of the destructive effects of sin, they can now establish their homes and their society on the principles of righteousness and honesty, and insure that God is worshipped and obeyed.

Climatically, however, things are different. Changes have taken place. There are now seasons (Gen. 8:22), and Noah and his sons must therefore learn when to sow their crops and when to reap. They must also adjust their lives to the heat of the sun's rays[7] and prepare for the cold of winter.

THE DEVIL'S VINEYARD

Just how soon after the flood Noah adds a vineyard to his farm lands is not stated. The biblical record is very brief. A certain amount of time must have elapsed for Noah's grandson, Canaan, has been born and is old enough to collaborate with his father in an act of disrespect (Gen. 9:22-25; Prov. 20:1; Hab. 2:15). While Noah is probably quite unaware of the effect wine will have on him, and perhaps has not had time to observe the changes which the seasons have made in the fermentation process of certain products, he becomes intoxicated. Unfortunately, connected with his drunkenness is also the sin of immodesty (Gen. 9:21). The Hebrew text clearly implies a deliberate act on Noah's part and not an unconscious effect of the wine upon him.

And as it was then, so it is now. Intemperance and impurity still are frequently linked together.

Noah's son, Ham, sees his father lying naked in his tent and surmises what has happened. He is perhaps accompanied by his son, Canaan. In any event, he tells his brothers what he has seen and they, with befitting respect, cover their father's body.

But what is Mrs. Noah's reaction to this situation? Does she tongue-lash her husband for his behavior, or is she supportive of him as a person realizing that the temptation to sin is common to us all? Once again, the Bible is silent. If Mrs. Noah was the pleasant, consistent, God-fearing wife she appears to be, then we may be sure she responded to her husband's sin with love and understanding. In the absence of any specific word, all we can do, however, is refer to other portions of Scripture to find out what our conduct should be in situations such as this. We do know that we all are engaged in a spiritual warfare (Eph. 6:10-18; 1 Peter 5:8). We also know that those who err should be restored in a spirit of meekness (Gal. 6:1).

In spite of this fall into sin, Noah regains his poise and continues to be the spiritual leader of his family. He lives for three hundred and fifty years after the Flood and on his death leaves behind him an example of a consistent life (Ezek. 14:14).

In reviewing the experiences of Noah and his wife, we are left to conclude with Henry Ward Beecher that "well-married a man is winged: ill-matched he is shackled." A man can have no possession more inspiring than a good wife and nothing more detrimental than a bad one. His wife is the single most important human being in his life.

Interaction

1. What were social conditions like for Noah and his family? How was Noah's wife able to live positively with unhappy situations? What influence did she exert on her sons as they were growing to manhood, and on her daughters-in-law after her sons married?

2. Noah is the second person in Scripture of whom it is recorded that he "walked with God" (Gen. 6:9). What does this imply? What relevance is there in his experience for us today?

3. "Patience" (or, in most revised translations, "perseverance") is a virtue which takes time to develop. In what specific ways was Noah called upon to exercise this trait? What does the Bible teach us regarding "divine delays"? (See Heb. 6:12; 10:36; 12:1; James 1:3, 4; 5:7-8; 10-11; 2 Peter 1:6; 2:20; Rev. 1:9; 2:2-3; etc.).

4. Some bumper stickers that have appeared recently read: HAPPINESS IS A NIGHT WITH YOUR FAMILY. What makes "family togetherness" threatening to some people? How can a "family night" be made really meaningful? Brainstorm for new ideas.

5. Why was Noah taken unawares when he drank the wine he had made from the grapes of his vineyard? From a consideration of Scriptures such as Proverbs 20:1; 21:17; 23:30; etc., (other references can be obtained from a concordance such as Strong's *Exhaustive Concordance of the Bible*) what should be the practice of Christian parents? What influence should they have on their children?

6

ENTER THE PROMISED LAND

Marriage is something you have to give your whole mind to.

—Henrik Ibsen

Genesis 12:1-9

In one of his books the famous Swiss physician, Dr. Paul Tournier, comments on the value of literature as a means of understanding human nature:

> What matters in this search for the person is not so much historical facts as the way in which we see and feel them . . . We learn as much about humanity from legends as from historical reports. They are a different reality, but a reality nevertheless. Indeed, they are a much more reliable document than the most learned history book. If we wish to understand man it is as important to read the *Iliad,* and the *Odyssey* . . . as philosophical, sociological, physiological or psychological treatises.[1]

One such story of antiquity from which we can learn important truths about ourselves concerns Pygmalion. Pygmalion was a sculptor. According to the Roman poet Ovid, when he attained marriageable age, Pygmalion began looking for a wife. The young women of his day so disgusted him that he resolved to remain single. Sensing the need of a female counterpart to make his life complete, he made an exquisite ivory statue. This magnificent sculpture embodied his concept of an ideal woman. As he gazed upon his handiwork, he fell in love with it, and, according to the story, would kiss it and caress it.

At a special festival held in honor of the goddess Aphrodite, Pygmalion prayed for a wife as lovely as his statue. When he returned home, Aphrodite gave life to the statue, and the beautiful young Galatea was soon married to Pygmalion.

Pygmalion, of course, illustrates the tendency of a young man to be attracted to a pretty girl while paying scant attention to the inner qualities which are all that will remain after her beauty has begun to fade.

In Ovid's story, Pygmalion was perfectly satisfied with Galatea, but was Galatea as satisfied with Pygmalion?

All of this leads us to ask, What are the characteristics which a woman finds desirable in a man? And how may these qualities contribute towards the stability, permanence and lasting enjoyment of their relationship?

WHAT ANALYSTS SAY

After considerable research, psychologists have come to the conclusion that every woman needs seven specific things in her husband, if she is to experience real fulfillment and enduring happiness.

(1) A woman needs to feel that she is wanted. She needs to feel special in her own home and loved and appreciated by her husband.

(2) A woman wants her husband to acknowledge her equality with him as a person and not be looked upon as someone of inferior worth and kept around to do the housekeeping and change the diapers on the children.

(3) A woman wants to feel secure. She wants to be able to trust her husband's judgment, leave certain decisions to him, and know that he is faithful to her.

(4) A woman also wants to feel fulfilled. This comes through the performance of the things God ordained her to do.

(5) A woman wants to be able to enjoy sex and not be looked upon as a sex object. She wants to be loved and sense her husband's loving care of her. She wants to be able to respond totally to him because she knows that he cares for her completely.

(6) Nearly every woman wants to bear children and, with her husband, enjoy loving involvement with them.

(7) Every woman wants companionship—the kind of complement-companionship which grows deeper and more intimate as the years go by.

Given these needs, what traits must a husband possess if he is to satisfy them? Did Abraham possess any intrinsic attributes which helped him meet Sarah's needs?*

The material on Abraham and Sarah (covering Genesis 12—23) is so vast that an entire book could easily be written on them.[2] We will concentrate solely on the relationship between Abraham and Sarah. We will seek to learn the secret of how he met her mental, emotional, and spiritual needs.

SOURCES OF TENSION

There is every indication in the Bible that Sarah's marriage to Abraham was a happy one. However, on taking a closer look at the circumstances she faced, we find that she left her home, family and friends in order to share a life of hardship with him (Gen. 12:1-3).

Ur (*Tell el-Maqaiyar,* "the Mound of Pitch"), the city where Sarah was born, was the leading commercial center of the day. It prided itself on its markets and stores. Imports of silks, perfumes, and jewelry delighted wealthy shoppers. The houses were large and spacious, and some homes that archaeologists have excavated had more than one level. It is possible that, having the benefits of wealth, Sarah lived in one of these.

It is while Sarah and Abraham are living in Ur (Acts 7:2), that Abraham has a profound spiritual experience. He is seventy-five years old at the time, and he and Sarah are childless (Gen. 11:30). The *"God of glory"* appears to him and turns him from the sensuous idolatry of his fathers (Josh. 24:2) to the worship of the one true God. God's words contained both a command and a promise: **"Leave your country, your kinsman, and your father's house, and go to a country that I will show you. I will make you a great nation, I will bless you and make your name great; and you will be a blessing. Those who bless you I will bless, and the one who curses you I will curse. And in you all the families of the earth shall be blessed"** (Gen. 12:1-3).

---

*In the early chapters of Genesis Abraham is called Abram, meaning "father," and Sarah, Sarai meaning "princess." For the sake of consistency they will be referred to as Abraham and Sarah.

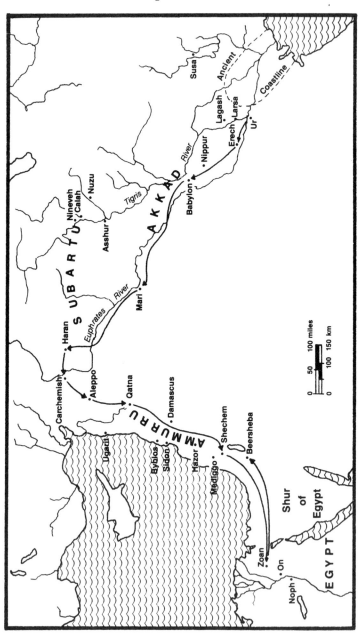

Route of Abraham

In obedience to God, Abraham leaves Ur for Haran. It is probable that Terah, Abraham and Sarah's father[3] (Gen. 20:12), is very old when the move is made. He may have taken ill en route for Haran (which, in Sumerian, means "caravan city" and was the melting pot of the races of the ancient Near East), and this may have led to their remaining in Haran until he died (Gen. 11:31-32).

As a merchant,[4] Abraham would have made the transition from Ur to the dusty, heavily trafficked streets of Haran much easier than Sarah. Gone now is the social sophistication of Ur. In its place is the oriental equivalent of cheap saloons, equally as cheap "motels," and the stench of countless camels.

With the passing of Terah, Abraham and Sarah move once more. Their lifestyle changes. Instead of a spacious burnt brick residence they now live in a tent (10' x 15', 3 x 4.6 meters) which is divided in half to separate woman's quarters from those of the men. Sarah's part of the tent also serves as a storage room for the cooking utensils. The desert floor with a mat and a few throw rugs becomes her bed. And the markets and stores, the refinements of civilization, her family and friends, are all left far behind. With her husband, she becomes a nomad, and the broad expanse of the Negev becomes her home.

What qualities did Abraham possess that made such hardships worthwhile? How did he hold Sarah's love so that hardly a complaint escaped her lips during more than sixty years of nomadic life? And what may husbands today learn from Abraham that will help them satisfy the needs of their wives?

THE CORE OF THINGS

Regardless of what others may say about the ideals of husband-wife relationships, the Bible begins with a man's relationship to God. This does not mean that a non-Christian couple cannot have a meaningful marriage. They can. However, with many marriages ending in divorce, and with some that do not, barely remaining intact, it is well for us to consider where God begins, and where He places the emphasis.

In Genesis 12 God reveals Himself and His will to Abraham; and Abraham responds. From this time onwards the focus of Abraham's life shifts. In place of his former self-centeredness he is now God-centered. The feelings of weakness and inadequacy and fear that caused him and his father (and those about them) to turn to idols for strength, is gone. He has a new focal point, and his life is now characterized by growth in the wisdom and knowledge of God.

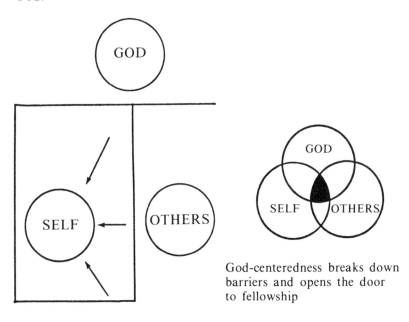

God-centeredness breaks down barriers and opens the door to fellowship

Self-centeredness sets up barriers in a relationship

Abraham also shares the revelation he has received with Sarah (Gen. 12:4-5; Heb. 11:8), and her faith comes to full maturity when she believes God's word concerning her and is given strength to conceive and bear a son (Heb. 11:11).

KEY FACTS

But why is a relationship with God so important?

When a person experiences the transforming love of God he comes to realize several things. First, he comes to appreciate how much God loves him. The more this truth lays hold of him, the more he is able to rejoice in his acceptance by God following the forgiveness of his sins (Eph. 1:6; 1 John 3:1). He delights in this forgiveness and can readily forgive any shortcomings his wife may have. His unconditional acceptance into the family of God (John 1:12) gives him love to enfold his wife (Eph. 5:25, 28).

The person who enters into the truth of what it means to belong to God's family (John 1:12) also becomes increasingly aware of his worth. He realizes that he has value as a person—for what he is rather than for the things he can do (Matt. 10:29-31). He has been made an heir of God and a joint-heir with Christ (Rom. 8:17; Titus 3:7). He need no longer strive to prove his worth through self-effort, nor need he castigate himself for his failures. He is free from the need to try and live up to some self-imposed and often unattainable standard. He is also free to accept his wife as a person of equal worth, a joint-heir of the grace of life (1 Peter 3:7), without expecting her to live up to some ideal which he may have.

Such a realization of the privilege of sonship will also equip him with a feeling of competence. The Holy Spirit indwells him (1 Cor. 4:20; Eph. 3:20), helps him with his relationships, and equips him to handle his responsibilities. He can do all things through Christ who strengthens him (Phil. 4:13).

There is no reason, therefore, why, when these truths are shared and acted on by both parties, their marriage should not be successful. Of course there will be times when they will fail. Realizing their proneness to sin, they should be quick to ask for forgiveness and always be ready to forgive each other (Matt. 6:14-15). Liberated from the shackles of self-centeredness, they are free to establish their relationship around a new center (Jer. 24:7; 31:31-34; Ezek. 11:19, 20). The love of God can then radiate through their home.

THIS THING CALLED LOVE

The change God brings about in the life of believers provides a foundation for the development of a healthy marriage. Instead of beginning with our inter-personal relationships, He begins with our relationship to Himself. When this is in its proper perspective (i.e., when our lives are

God-centered) we can begin to develop a meaningful relationship with one another. Love—the love which God gives us for each other, in which we seek each other's highest good—is the only *positive* relational emotion. The other relationship emotions—hostility (anger), guilt, and fear—are destructive of our relationships. When we respond to God's love with love (1 John 4:19) we begin to reverse the cycle of the negative emotions in our lives.

But how is this worked out in practice?

In First Peter 3:7, the apostle writes: *"You husbands should live with your wives in an understanding* [considerate] *way, as with a weaker vessel, since she is a woman; and grant her honor as a fellow-heir of the grace of life, so that your prayers may not be hindered."*

A woman is more finely strung than a man. Her husband should therefore study her disposition, know her temperament, be considerate of her, and insure that she feels secure. The conversations of Abraham and Sarah recorded in the Bible provide us with good illustrations of this important truth. Take, for example, the one in Genesis 16. After Sarah has given her servant, Hagar, to Abraham, Hagar conceives. Sarah senses that she is despised. She feels humiliated. She therefore turns on her husband and blames him for what has happened (Gen. 16:5). In actual fact, what Sarah and Abraham have done is quite in keeping with the culture of their day.[5] It would have been easy for Abraham to defend himself against his wife's accusation. Instead, he replies with tact and discretion, and avoids a rift in their relationship.

Such ability is developed only through the careful study of the nature of one's wife. And no man can claim to be a good husband who has not taken time to study his spouse's personality and understand her special needs.

Realizing that a wife needs to feel special, a husband should insure that she receives the kind of attention that communicates how much she means to him. It may be through flowers, an evening out together, or just the way he takes her in his arms and says, "I love you." Such assurances will eliminate the need one woman felt when she sought out a marriage counselor. In the first session she stated tearfully, "When we first married Johnny treated me like a queen. Now he barely notices me. When he comes home for an evening he slumps down in a chair in the den to read the newspaper. And after supper he watches TV. We have no life together."

Perhaps this is why the apostle Peter insisted that husbands should "live *with* their wives"—sharing common interests, engaging in common activities, and not merely residing as boarders under the same roof. Living *with* one's wife involves cultivating the love-relationship which first brought them together. We cannot imagine Abraham and Sarah being so busy that, in the heat of the day, they did not take time to rest and converse (Gen. 18:1-6); or, in the cool of the evening, enjoy one another's company around the fire.

Of course, there are some husbands whose business schedule necessitates that they work at night and sleep during the day, or be away from home for periods of time, or whose studies require that they spend most of their time "in the books." But even in these situations quality time devoted solely to their wives with no interruptions permitted, can make up for what may be lacking in quantity.

There is also something in Peter's statement *"since she is a woman"* which calls to mind the apostle Paul's words in Colossians 3:19. He said, *"Husbands, love your wives, and do not be embittered against them."* At first glance we may question, What do these statements have in common? What do they mean? The answer is not hard to find. Because of the stress and strain of everyday life, the unfulfilled hopes, and the abrasive attitude of other people, it is easy to become frustrated. We seldom show our resentment in public, but frequently flare up at home. The "provocation" may be a minor one, the result of a difference in temperament, and because we may not give our wives the love and under-standing they deserve, we release our resentment on them. They, therefore, are the ones who suffer. Peter reminds us that the wife is the *"weaker vessel"* and worthy of more consideration instead of less.

In the relationship of Abraham and Sarah we find that he exercised this kind of understanding. God had promised that His blessing would run through their seed, Isaac, the son of their old age (Gen. 17:15-21). Several years after Isaac had been born, God appeared to Abraham one night and told him to offer Isaac as a burnt offering (Gen. 22:1-8). When Abraham awoke the next morning, he did as the Lord had commanded him. His relationship with the Lord was real. He had walked by faith for many years. He knew he could trust God's promise to him regarding Isaac. *Fully confident that he and Isaac would return* (Gen. 22:5), he set out for Mount Moriah. The record implies that he did not tell Sarah the purpose of the journey. He was considerate of her. He knew they would both come home.

Most wives would want to be in on a decision as momentous as this. Between Abraham and Sarah there was evidently such confidence that each knew they could trust the other. Such interpersonal assurance takes time to develop. It is the exact opposite of those situations where the one wants to know all that the other has been doing. Sarah trusted Abraham. Abraham trusted God. Therefore, why cause Sarah any unnecessary concern?

And for her part, Sarah was content to leave certain things to the discretion of her husband. He had surrounded her with such love and understanding for so many years that doubt and suspicion had been excluded from their relationship. All of this was possible because they had made God the center of their lives.

WHAT'S TO FOLLOW

In our next chapter we will focus on some additional traits Abraham possessed. Sufficient to say at this time that when a man is before God, that he is in his home; that and no more. No man can expect to be a consistently good husband and exercise proper headship unless he has the kind of vital relationship with God that Abraham had. This took Abraham's actions (particularly the sacrificing of Isaac) outside the realm of chance, for he walked by faith and had for many years made the Lord the focal point of his life.

Interaction

1. As you read through Genesis 11:29—12:9 (keeping in mind that Abraham and Sarah were half-brother and sister, Gen. 20:12), what particular problems might have

developed in the marital relationship of Abraham (Abram) and Sarah (Sarai)? Make a list of these.

2. In what ways might the problems Sarah faced (in #1 above) have been taken care of when God became the focal point of both of their lives? What differences would a sense of belonging, worth, and confidence make in their relationship? Describe how these principles apply to the situations we face today as these apply (a) to husbands, and (b) to wives.

3. How would you define love? In what ways does your concept of love for your husband or wife help you overcome the negative feelings of hostility (anger), guilt, and fear?

4. What feelings of Sarah's are in evidence in Genesis 16:5?* How did Abraham handle them (see Prov. 15:1)?

5. Brainstorm 1 Peter 3:7 for the specific ways in which husbands might take the initiative in cultivating their wives. Write down these ideas. Which ones do you think should be implemented first? Why? Which ones do you think your wives would respond to quickest? Where do you plan to begin? How will you proceed?

---

*The *Code of Hammurabi*—the legislation governing the people of Mesopotamia shortly after the time of Abraham and Sarah—protected the rights of a slave used to raise children for the husband of their mistress. Sarah's conduct in Genesis 16:6b violated Hagar's rights and shows how deep was her anger.

7

SARAH'S "PYGMALION"

The foundation upon which any happy home is built is the trust and affection a man has for his wife and the high regard in which she holds her husband.
—Anonymous

Genesis 12:10-13:4

A successful marriage generally passes through three stages. First, there is the *mutual enjoyment* phase. The couple is on their honeymoon and caught up in the ecstasy of being together. They delight in their new oneness and seem to observers to be inseparable.

As the honeymoon ends and the couple return home, a change of emphasis takes place. They must now shoulder the responsibilities of everyday life. It is at this time that the period of *mutual adjustment* begins.[1] The success or failure of their marriage will depend on their maturity, the way they develop true unity, and their sexual compatibility.

Finally, after many years, there comes the *mutual fulfillment* stage. This stage is the result of the development of their commitment to each other. For its maturing to take place, there must, of necessity, be the sharing of a common purpose and the uniting of their wills as they work to achieve common goals. In a Christian marriage this includes making the Lord the center of their lives.

Our concern in this chapter will be to concentrate attention on those characteristics which, at least from the husband's point of view, contribute to the mutual adjustment and personal growth of the marriage. As we do, we will look at another vignette in the lives of Abraham and Sarah.

NOBODY'S PERFECT

Our story is brief. It tells of a severe famine in Canaan. Abraham decides to journey down to Egypt. As he and Sarah are about to enter Egypt (probably as they approach the "Wall of the Ruler"[2]) Abraham says to Sarah: *"See now, I know that you are a woman of beautiful appearance;[3] and it will come about when the Egyptians see you, that they will say, 'This is his wife'; and they will kill me, but they will let you live. Please say that you are my sister[4] so that it may go well with me because of you, and I may live on account of you."*

It is quite evident that Abraham is motivated by fear. He seizes on a half truth (Gen. 20:12) by which to deceive the Egyptians.

Commentators have severely criticized Abraham for making this proposal to Sarah. They believe he placed her in a vulnerable position in order to save himself. Dr. William Blaikie says:

> Neither Godward nor manward does he appear in a favourable light . . . (His suggestion) was the fruit of unbelief, of forgetfulness of the promise, 'I will bless them that bless thee, and curse them that curseth thee' . . . To propose that Sarah should commit an act of deceit was bad enough, but to propose what would humiliate her, with a view to her husband's safety, was even worse.[5]

Such a view of Abraham's conduct exhibits a proneness to judge his action by western standards. Those who condemn him presume that he completely disregarded Sarah's safety and moral integrity.

The Bible plainly implies that Abraham was goaded by fear, but does this mean that he was not also motivated by love for Sarah? Isn't it possible that there may have been something in his suggestion that we have overlooked?

In actual fact, the plan Abraham devised is a masterpiece of ingenuity. In his society, anyone wishing to marry a woman must, of necessity, negotiate with her father, or, if he is dead, with her brother (comp. Gen. 24:28-31, 50-53). In planning to pass off Sarah as his sister—a move which God's word records without approval—Abraham takes advantage of this custom. His scheme is a shrewd one. Anyone wishing to marry Sarah will have to make the arrangments through him.[6] He can draw out the negotiations, ask for a prohibitive dowry, thwart the would-be suitor, so that he becomes discouraged and tires of his plans of marriage, or, if all else fails, he and his servants can

> Fold up their tents, like the Arabs,
> and as silently steal away.

The advantage of Abraham's plan is that both he and Sarah will be preserved alive. And when the flap of his tent is closed at night, Sarah has only to raise the curtain separating her quarters from his, and they can be together.

Abraham's plan miscarries in Egypt, but only because the Egyptians do not observe the same social customs as the people of the Fertile Crescent. This setback does not prevent Abraham and Sarah from practicing the same deceptive charade in other places—over a twenty-five-year period—and with apparent success (Gen. 20:11-13).

Abraham's purpose—not his lapse of faith—is the important principle for us to notice. His motive was one of real love for Sarah. And Sarah's response shows her love for her husband.

Real love for one another is the basis of mutual adjustment in marriage. Without it selfishness, pride, or arrogance can easily begin to dominate the relationship. When this happens it is hard for the proper changes to take place. Whatever we may say about Abraham's proposal to Sarah, there can be no doubt that she felt loved and wanted.

TUNNEL VISION

Having dealt with what happened on the way to Egypt we must still ask and answer the question, Why did Abraham doubt the promise God had made to him (Gen. 12:1-3)? What really led up to his lapse of faith?

As we look for the solution to Abraham's conduct we are compelled to turn once more to Genesis 20. From this chapter two important truths emerge. The fear which prompted his deception was the result (1) of the godlessness of the people about him, v. 11, and (2) his feeling of aloneness or isolation, v. 13.

When God called Abraham to leave his homeland for Canaan, Abraham left behind his relatives and friends. This meant that in a crisis he could not turn to them for help. Humanly speaking, he was alone. He was a stranger (a *"wanderer from his father's house"*) in a strange land. He felt insecure. He lacked the sense of belonging, worth and competence (that we discussed in our previous chapter) to handle a crisis.

With this in mind, let us look at the events of chapter 12 from Abraham's perspective.

As Abraham enters Canaan he looks for a place in which to settle. He passes through the land to Shechem. This is the land God has promised to give him, and yet he feels he does not belong. The Canaanites live there. He decides to journey on. He comes to "the oak of Moreh" and there builds an altar. For some reason he still feels uneasy and journeys on to Bethel. But things still are not right and he moves again, this time to the Negev.

Abraham is just beginning to settle down when there is a severe famine in the land. His camels, flocks and herds are threatened. This increases his feelings of insecurity. If he should lose these he will have nothing left. Instead of trusting in the Lord, he does what other herders are doing; he goes down to Egypt where the annual inundation of the Nile River almost always assures a harvest.

But now he faces another problem. The things he has heard about the Egyptians fill him with fear. He assumes, and perhaps with good reason,[7] that the people will do him harm rather than help him. Instead of placing his confidence in the Lord he decides to trust in himself and his own abilities. Filled with misgivings (or fear)[8] he asks Sarah to collaborate with him in a willful act of deception.

It is well for us to remember that when we lack a sense of belonging, worth, and competence, we feel insecure; and when we feel insecure, it is very easy for us to give way to fear. In order for us to understand the biblical narrative, let us pause for a moment to analyze fear.

Fear arises in our hearts when we attribute to a person, event, or thing two primary attributes which properly belong to God: *almightiness* (the power to take away our self-direction or autonomy), and *impendency* (the power to do us harm). Because of God's nature He has the right to command our obedience. He does not do so because He desires our willing service. He also has the right to punish us. However, He prefers to deal with us in love and exercise His power as Judge only when compelled to do so. When caught in the web of fear we attribute to someone or something these characteristics, and the result is a state of acute anxiety.

Different people handle fear in different ways. They may struggle against it, retreat from it, or surrender to it. Or, they may do all three.

In our story Abraham capitulates before his fears, and it takes the failure of his plan and the stern rebuke of the king of Egypt to show him the error of his ways. He then returns to Canaan and the place where he had built an altar to the Lord (Gen. 13:1-3). There he renews the vital link of fellowship with God which was missing while he was in Egypt. And with this strengthening he can face the remaining period of the famine. The test of his faith is not reduced, only changed. Before, his flocks and herds were few and the anticipation period of the famine long. Now, *"he is rich in livestock"* and the famine just as severe.

THE ONLY REAL SOLUTION

But this is not the only time Abraham is filled with fear. Some years later, after Lot has chosen to live in Sodom, four kings of the East[9] will attack the cities of the plain (Gen. 14). The kings of these cities will be defeated, and they and their subjects will be taken captive. Lot will be among them. On hearing of the overthrow of these cities, Abraham will muster his men and pursue the invaders. He will stage a successful surprise attack and rescue Lot and the people (Gen. 14:13-16). After the flush of victory has passed, Abraham will experience misgivings (Gen. 15:1). He will fear reprisal. He will realize his vulnerability. He will think that as soon as these kings learn who it was who routed them, they will come looking for him.

It is when these thoughts will disturb his peace of heart and mind that God will appear to him and say:

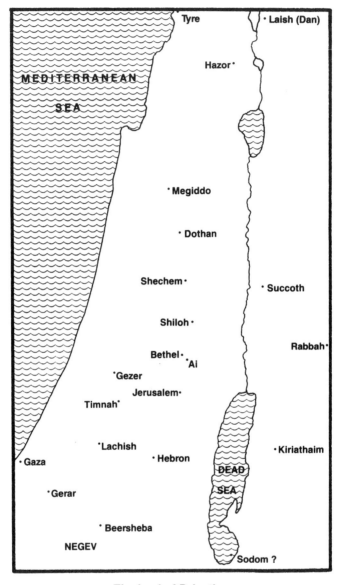

The land of Palestine

Do not fear, Abram,
I am your shield . . . .

It is in this assurance that God gives to Abraham that we find the solution to the problem of fear. The only way to successfully resolve our fears is to commit ourselves and our fears to the Lord (Ps. 55:22; 1 Pet. 5:7; *cf.,* Rom. 8:15). By living in submission to His will, we will enjoy the security and peace we otherwise would forfeit (Matt. 11:28-30; Jas. 1:25). When we do those things that please Him, He makes even our enemies live at peace with us (Prov. 16:7).

AREAS OF VULNERABILITY

Realizing that even a man such as Abraham failed, is instructive, for we can learn from his experience. But what, may we ask, was Sarah's reaction to his proposal?

Abraham's lapse of faith does not excuse his sin, but it does correct the notion of some wives that their husbands should be free from error. When a husband fails to fulfill some preconceived standard of perfection, his wife may begin to badger him. She may unconsciously show that she expects more from him by constantly nagging him about something. "Why can't you be thoughtful and considerate; you know, the kind of person pastor was talking about on Sunday morning." Or, "Why can't you fix the leaking faucet? My dad always took care of the things about the house that needed fixing." Or, "Why don't you manage our finances better? I never hear Diane complaining about being overdrawn at the bank."

Let's be frank, husbands have shortcomings! These areas of real or imagined failure should be discussed openly and objectively. Then a plan of action should be mutually agreed upon and implemented in a way that allows for growth in the relationship. And all the while the wife can be lovingly supportive of her less-than-perfect husband.

Is this what Sarah did? What we are not told in Genesis 12 is stated explicitly for us in 1 Peter 3:1-6.

FACE-SAVING FORMULA

There can be no doubt that Sarah went along with Abraham's proposal. But what was her attitude in doing so?

Peter points to Sarah as an example of an ideal woman[10] and says that she *"obeyed Abraham, calling him lord"* (1 Peter 3:6a). By this he means that she was supportive of him, even when he was wrong.

What type of response did this produce in Abraham? By acquiescing to his suggestion she preserved his self-esteem. This made it easy for him to relate to her in love. Their relationship was not strained. And when he was rebuked for his deception by Pharaoh and had to leave Egypt in disgrace, there was no "I told you so," but rather the same tender solicitude that made it easy for him to return to Bethel and be restored to fellowship with God (Gen. 12:18-13:4).

There are some wives, however, who feel that to follow the Bible's teaching on "submission" to their husbands will lead to their becoming twentieth-century "slaves." They believe that such a practice will deprive them of a mind or will of their own. When they are forced to grapple with passages of Scripture such as this one in First Peter, they resort to the explanation that it describes a culturally conditioned phenomenon which finds no parallel in our society today. But those who make much of the cultural conditions of the ancient Near East often pass over the fact, that the things recorded in God's Word were written for our learning (Rom. 15:4) and that events of the past are designed by God to serve as examples for us (1 Cor. 10:11). They contain important *principles,* and these principles apply to people of any day and age. This is what makes the Bible both timeless in its teaching and relevant in its application!

A favorite "proof text" of those who pass over the teaching of the Old Testament is Galatians 3:28. There, we are told that we are all one in Christ. This verse, however, does not say that the distinctions of sex are erased at the time of conversion. A woman continues to be a woman and a man continues to be a man. What Paul is saying is that there is equality of privilege. Men do not enjoy greater prerogatives than women, for in God's sight we are all one in Christ.

To those wives who lament that their husbands will then take advantage of them, there is the example of Sarah. Her submission to Abraham did not cause him to treat her like a chattel. Instead, it opened the way for him to relate to her in a loving and affectionate manner. He felt free to dote over her, court her as he did before they were married, and insure that she was treated with respect.

It is of interest for us to notice that the word translated "honor" in 1 Peter 3:7 is translated "precious" in 1 Peter 1:19. Not only is a man's wife his "queen," but when she helps preserve his fragile ego, he is able to treat her as someone of infinite worth!

SPONTANEOUS REALIGNMENT

Don and Alice had been married for nearly fourteen years. In recent months, when in the company of men from his office, Don had begun hinting in a lighthearted way that being single again would be preferable to having to put up with Alice's constant bickering.

One morning Don and Alice had their daily argument early. It began when they got up (or perhaps it had just been carried over from the night before). Anyway, Don left the house with his breakfast still on his plate. He was fully determined that this time he would obtain a legal separation.

Shortly before noon that morning Don received a phone call from the hospital. Alice had apparently gone to the supermarket before going to visit her mother. A truck had run a red light, their car had been crumpled like a matchbox, paramedics had had to cut away part of the car to get Alice out, and she was now in the hospital awaiting surgery. Would he come and sign the papers?

Later that week Don confided that in those moments after receiving the call from the hospital he realized how much Alice really meant to him. "Oh God, please don't let her die!" he prayed over and over as he drove to the hospital. Then, after signing the papers, he waited and waited. Finally, after what seemed like a millennium, he was allowed to see her. "I wanted to ask her forgiveness for my display of temper and tell her that I loved her," he told us, "but she was so heavily sedated that I do not know if she heard me."

The next few weeks were filled with bittersweet for Don and Alice. There were visits to the hospital, love and tears, the opening of channels of communication, and the evidence of personal awareness for past mistakes. Alice underwent two more operations, and even after returning home spent several months convalescing. During all this time the love and unity they had once known came to full bloom.

A year later Don and Alice visited us in our home. "It took a near-fatal accident to show us how much we meant to each other," Don admitted. And Alice confided, "It also demonstrated what tender love and consideration for each other could do in our marriage!" It had been a year of mutual adjustment for them. They had each come to the place where they were willing to acknowledge their errors and do something to put things right. Don found that he could love Alice freely, and she learned that devotion to and involvement with Don in what he was doing insured that he would give her the position of honor in his life. In the course of time Don was able to develop an in-depth understanding of Alice, listen to what she had to say, pay attention to the things that interested her, become sensitive to her changing moods, discuss with her any problems she might be facing, and learn to understand her. This was not always easy. It took time. The benefits, however, amply repaid his efforts and the result was a renewed sense of the blessing of the Lord on their lives.

Interaction

1. Discuss some of the issues (as openly and as impartially as circumstances will allow) which, as far as you are concerned, have constituted problem areas of adjustment in your marriage. How have you and your spouse worked on them? What different approaches might you now take in light of this chapter?
2. Consider some of the things—people, circumstances, events—that cause us to feel anxiety (i.e., fear) such as loss of friends, job or health, bad news, earthquakes, or even travel by plane. What makes our fears so powerful? How may Abraham's experiences help you overcome them?
3. Some wives expect their husbands to turn in a "perfect performance" in virtually all areas of life. Why? Could this be as a result of having (a) idolized their father and expect their husband to measure up to this internalized image of perfection, (b) some unrealized expectations in their

marriage that they hold their husband accountable for, or (c) that they are trying to suppress some personal immaturity and therefore project their failure onto someone else (i.e., their husbands)? What are some of the ways they can adjust to a less-than-perfect mate?

4. Discuss some of the fears wives experience (e.g., fear that their husbands will take advantage of them if they acknowledge his headship; fear that an unsaved husband will not be saved unless they witness to him; fear that the inevitable aging process will render them unattractive; etc.) alluded to in 1 Peter 3:1-6.

5. How may spiritual values be shared by a Christian couple?

8

MUTUAL BENEFITS

*Ideally, the marital relationship is one where the
independence is equal, the dependence mutual, and the
obligation reciprocal.*

—L. K. Anspacher

Genesis 18:1-8

We began our discussion of the marriage of Abraham and
Sarah with an analysis of the specifics wives desire most in
their husbands. We found that while they need to feel wanted,
be acknowledged by their husbands as equals, feel secure,
experience fulfillment, enjoy sex, participate in loving
involvement with their family (i.e., husband and children),
and delight in the benefits of companionship, not every
husband is capable of meeting these needs. The explanation
for this general inability of husbands to satisfy all the desires
of their wives is not hard to find. Dr. Gary Strauss relates it to
the Fall.

Modern psychology clearly recognizes three psychological
needs as basic to all mankind. They are the need to belong (to
love and be loved), the need for feelings of self worth (to accept
and value oneself), and the need for confidence (to feel capable
of handling one's environment). How beautifully were these
needs met in the Garden of Eden. There was no question as to
Adam's and Eve's belonging. Their very reason for being was to
have fellowship with God, and they were literally "made for
each other." Being the apex of God's creation and having the
Garden ideally suited to them were clear indications of their
worth in God's sight. Finally, their ability to carry out their
responsibility for dressing and keeping the Garden, coupled
with the friendly response of the Garden and its animal
inhabitants to their efforts, could do nothing but insure an
unquestioned confidence. Adam and Eve were totally secure.

How greatly the Fall changed all this. Suddenly Adam's and Eve's relationship with God was broken, and they were soon cast out of the Garden. No longer did they belong. As their place of honor was lost, they began to question their worth. Confidence was shattered as their environment became hostile to them. No longer were their basic psychological needs being met so unconditionally. From perfect harmony to painful conflict in barely a moment of time! Their total security had vanished, replaced by an anxious insecurity. Whereas God had been the focal point in their lives, now self became the center— a weak, dependent, anxious and insecure self—a self in conflict with God and His divine plan and purpose, vainly attempting to meet its own needs.[1]

Insecurity produces fear, and fear impairs our ability to initiate proper action. This is why in His dealings with mankind (and illustrated for us in Abraham), God begins by emphasizing the spiritual dimension—the only way a person may feel completely secure. From this premise a man can begin to relate in a wholesome way to his wife (and, of course, to others as well). And when situations arise in which he may sense a lack of belonging, worth, or competence, he has only to reflect on his standing before God for the practical impact of these truths to offset any negative influence.

Following the initial study of Abraham's relationship to God, we considered the fact that no husband is perfect. For wives to set, and then expect their husbands to reach, an unattainable standard is to invite trouble. On the other hand, for them to be lovingly supportive of their all-too-human mates is to fulfill the biblical model.

WALLS OF LOVE

We now consider the ways in which a husband may be *lovingly innovative.* Virtually every reference to Abraham in the Bible shows him either responding promptly to some message from the Lord, or sizing up a situation and taking appropriate action. In either case (and allowing for occasional lapses of faith) it demonstrates his security—his confidence in God and personal reliance.

As we pursue the story of Abraham and Sarah it is interesting to notice (1) the different ways in which Abraham took appropriate action, and (2) to observe Sarah's response.

When we were first introduced to Abraham, it was to learn of God's appearance to him (Gen. 12:1-4; Acts 7:2-4), and his prompt obedience to the Lord's command. He left his family and friends for an undisclosed destination. And when there was a famine in the land to which God had led him, he made a decision to go to Egypt. Later on, after returning from Egypt, when there was dissension between his herdsmen and those of his nephew, Lot, he sized up the situation and suggested a solution (Gen. 13:7-12).

In the course of time when the kings of the East invaded the land, overran Sodom and Gomorrah, and captured Lot, Abraham took decisive action and rescued his nephew (Gen. 14:1-16). On his return from this successful campaign, he encountered Melchizedek, king of Salem. With true spiritual insight he recognized Melchizedek to be a priest of *El Elyon,* "God Most High," and voluntarily gave him the tithe of all he possessed (Gen. 14:17-20). He had no sooner left Melchizedek's presence than an opportunity presented itself whereby he could enrich himself with the spoils of war. He declined, not because he could not take advantage of an opportunity, but on account of principle (Gen. 14:21-24).

And when certain "travellers"[2] visit him and tell him what lies in store for Sodom and Gomorrah, Abraham, of his own accord, will pray for the righteous people in those wicked cities (Gen. 18:22-33).

Finally, after more than sixty years in Canaan, when news will reach Abraham (who is away from home checking on his flocks and herds) that Sarah has died in Hebron, he will go and mourn for her. He will have occasion to think back on the life they have shared together. He will also have cause to praise God for the way He has fulfilled His promises to them, and thank Him for the love, loyalty and devotion of his beloved wife. And after weeping for Sarah, he will rise up to do what needs to be done (Gen. 23:3-4).

In all of his actions Abraham shows himself to be motivated from within. He is able to make decisions and take appropriate action without waiting for external circumstances to compel him to act.

A TIME TO ACT

It is this ability to be an innovative leader which is of great importance to the husband-wife relationship. It has been said that "if the husband has a good 'self-starter,' the wife doesn't have to be a 'crank'." The husband and father should be the initiator of family discussions, devotions, and discipline. He should be *the* leader in the home. This kind of loving involvement takes considerable pressure off the wife.

It is evident that Abraham carried over the ability to size up a situation and take appropriate action into his home. Sarah felt secure in their relationship. She realized from long experience that she could trust her husband. He was lovingly innovative.

One way a husband can be a loving initiator in the home is to let his wife in on his life, his plans, his ambitions. Abraham did. He shared with Sarah his desire for a son. Such was Sarah's response that when *"it ceased to be with her after the manner of women,"* she persuaded him to take her maid, Hagar, so that she might have a son by her servant (Gen. 16:1-3).[3] Her action illustrates the principle that when a wife feels loved and secure (as a result of her husband's innovative leadership), she will respond to him in positive ways, encourage him in what he is doing, and even do things for him at great cost to herself.

MARITAL DIFFICULTIES

When a husband is not lovingly innovative—when he is tardy in initiating communication, expressing his love, administering discipline,[4] providing for the needs of the family, and taking the lead in spiritual matters—his wife may begin to feel neglected and unloved. She may then begin to draw him into her life to reassure herself that he still cares for her. She may remind him of the things around the house that need fixing, or complain about how she feels.

Regardless of the way in which these "games"[5] are played, all the husband senses in these reproaches is that he is inadequate. He can never measure up to her standards, do all the things she wants done, or supply her with what she needs if she is to feel right and be happy. The impression he gets is that she is always nagging him about something. By way of contrast, some attractive "young thing" at the office is prepared to listen to his problems, be supportive of his ideas, and is not continuously lamenting his inability to do this or that. The result: he may begin to spend more time "at the office" than he does at home.[6] And the reason? A bitter cycle has developed in his home. The less leadership he assumes in the home the more his wife tries to draw him into her life; but in all the wrong ways. He begins to respond to her belittling with anger and resentment. She then tries harder. He becomes more and more "uptight," is filled with bitterness and more inclined to be resentful. And so the vicious cycle continues.

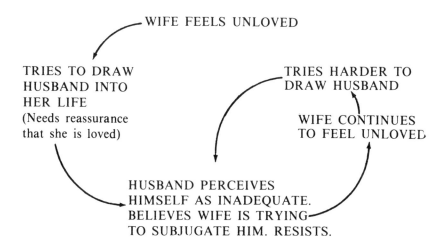

WIFE FEELS UNLOVED

TRIES TO DRAW
HUSBAND INTO
HER LIFE
(Needs reassurance
that she is loved)

TRIES HARDER TO
DRAW HUSBAND

WIFE CONTINUES
TO FEEL UNLOVED

HUSBAND PERCEIVES
HIMSELF AS INADEQUATE.
BELIEVES WIFE IS TRYING
TO SUBJUGATE HIM. RESISTS.

BRIGHT FUTURE

When the husband shoulders his responsibility as a *loving innovator* in the home and shows his love for his wife by doing things for her, she will be free to respond to him as a *willing supporter.* In this role she is able to build up and encourage her husband. Unfortunately, some wives have become so "miffed" over the neglect they feel that all thought of "building up" their husbands is dismissed from their minds. They shrink from being supportive and feel that the only way they can keep their husband manageable is by continuously tearing away at his sense of esteem. They fear that if they begin to support him he might think that he's reached the stage of perfection. They fail to realize that by tearing away at their husband's self-image they are forcing him to continuously defend himself and are hindering, rather than helping, his personal growth and development.

The real need of a wife—as outlined in our last chapter in the illustration of Sarah—is to be supportive of and responsive to her less-than-perfect husband (Prov. 31:12). This should not be done out of "fear" (1 Peter 3:6) that he will take advantage of her, for through her loving support of him the destructive cycle can be broken. Her husband will then find it easier to share things with her. When this happens he will begin to demonstrate more initiative in the home and the result will be greater harmony in their relationship.

CLUTTERED WITH CONFLICTS

There are three vitally important areas of married life where the loving innovation of the husband and the supportive encouragement of the wife are absolutely essential: money, in-laws, and sexual intimacy.

Money may be regarded as a necessary evil (Matt. 6:21; 1 Tim. 6:9-10). We need it to survive, but the urge to be rich or financially independent can easily blot out other considerations and blight a marriage. And even in those homes where the husband and wife are frugal and, as far as possible, stay out of debt, money matters can become a source of contention.

Harry and Inez were new believers and were growing in the faith. They gave a nominal amount to the church each week. One Sunday their pastor challenged the congregation with the need to support a couple who had volunteered for missionary service. He mentioned the "tithe" as belonging to the Lord. Harry went home to find out what a "tithe" was. When he learned that it represented one-tenth of all he earned (Deut. 14:22-25), the amount seemed unusually large. He and Inez, however, decided to try to tithe. They succeeded for two months, then Inez found that she was pregnant. Now the money they were giving to the church seemed even larger and more important to her than before. It was hard for her to be a "cheerful giver" (2 Cor. 9:7). Harry was in favor of trusting the Lord, she was all for paying off their debts and preparing for the arrival of their baby.

In facing this situation, Harry and Inez found it necessary to do some old-fashioned budgeting. They needed to discuss matters fully, decide on what the Lord wanted them to do, and order their priorities. This wasn't easy. There were times during their discussion when Harry felt like "laying down the law," and on more than one occasion Inez felt like crying because she felt she could not win the debate with Harry. However, by facing the problem realistically, Inez was able to be lovingly supportive of her husband.

The problems of Harry and Inez were different from those of Janet and Tom. They had married while Tom was in grad school. Because of their financial situation they had moved in with Tom's mother, a widow. Janet had worked before their baby arrived and, seeing Mrs. Walters only in the evenings, limited their contact. Now, however, Janet spent all day with her mother-in-law, and problems developed. When their baby was asleep Mrs. Walters would pick it up. She was sure the baby needed his diapers changed, or had cried, or wanted to be reassured that someone was there. Janet protested, but Mrs. Walters acted as though she never even heard her. Janet told Tom how she felt, but due to their financial situation and the advanced nature of his doctoral studies, he did nothing.

One day Janet exploded. She told Mrs. Walters what she thought of her, picked up her baby and, calling a taxi, went to her mother's. "Mother Walters won't leave me alone. She wants to manage everything. I've spoken to Tom but he won't support me. He gives in to her—everybody does."

Tom faced a dilemma that night. His mother, of course, justified herself. Tom, however, was finally goaded into taking appropriate action. He found an inexpensive and unpretentious place for him and Janet to live in, and Janet gladly returned to him. His studies suffered because he had to take an extra part-time job to pay "for the roof over their heads," but even the extra year he had to spend in the university was more than compensated for by the loving attention of his wife.

Problems in marriage, if not corrected, sooner or later make their presence felt in the marriage bed. In the case of Frank and Candie their difficulties came after nearly fifteen years of marriage. They were vaguely dissatisfied with their relationship, had become grouchy, and each, at different times, had engaged in "sexual politics."

The problem was that Candie felt trapped by the monotony of suburban living. The children were in school most of the day and did not need her as formerly. She felt unfulfilled and began craving for involvement in something more meaningful, and exciting. Then she would think of Frank. The very thought of his deteriorating, late-thirties "lack-of-interest-in-things" angered her. He was so unromantic, so "blah."

But Frank was having problems too. His former supervisor had been promoted and his new boss was unable to command the respect of the men as his predecessor had done. The team spirit was gone and the workers were dissatisfied. Should he look around for something else? Frank wasn't sure.

In the midst of these tensions there were also problems with the children: Frank Jr., thirteen, and Cathie, eleven. Candie left all the disciplining to him, but was so permissive herself that he felt alienated from his own family, because he was the only one issuing reprimands and "holding the line" on behavior. And on top of it all, Candie kept nagging him about being sexually unresponsive. The truth of the matter was that he was too angry to be responsive.

Finally, Frank and Candie decided to see a licensed marriage and family counselor. He helped them explore their areas of discontent. In the process they learned how to talk over the way they felt, just as they had done in the early years of their marriage. Frank came to understand the need for his loving innovation, and, after a few false starts he was surprised to find Candie responsive. As a result of this experience, they both realized that a healthy relationship requires continuous, undivided attention.

Interaction

In Genesis 18:1-8 Sarah unexpectedly has guests for dinner.
1. Discuss the different kinds of reactions Abraham might

have received from his wife when he imposed on her to bake "bread cakes" over an open fire in the heat of the day.

2. Abraham's politeness and courtesy (v. 2), activity (vv. 6-7), conviviality and respect (v. 8), are indicative of a well-ordered, generous disposition. Assuming that Abraham treated his wife in the same tender manner, what kind of husband would he have made? Why?

3. Some people, men as well as women, are two-faced. They can be charming and delightful (or compliant) in the presence of others but are wretched and distasteful (or obstinate) when alone with their spouses. Do you think Abraham and Sarah were like this? What evidence is there to support your viewpoint?

4. Abraham's actions in verse 6 are balanced by his own activity in verse 7. What does this teach us about loving innovation?

5. Sarah's prompt response to what might have been considered an imposition shows the beauty of her character and the quality of her relationship with her husband. How may modern "daughters of Sarah" (1 Peter 3:6) develop the same spontaneous distinctives?

9

WORTHY OF PRAISE

Rare is the union of beauty and virtue.
　　　　　　　　　　　—Juvenal

The influence of the greatest personal beauty, unless supported by force of character, is ever short-lived.
　　　　　　　　　　　—Harriet Martineau

Genesis 18:9-15; 21:1-7

A wise mother was giving counsel to her son as to the kind of wife he should choose. She concluded her admonition by saying, *"Charm can be deceptive and beauty doesn't last, but a woman who reverences the LORD shall be greatly praised"* (Prov. 31:30). She knew that a man is instinctively drawn to an attractive woman and therefore recommended that her son look for those qualities in his wife which improve with age.

From our study of the book of Genesis we know that even at age sixty Sarah was alluring. She undoubtedly looked after herself, and even when deprived of access to the stores and markets (due to the fact that she and Abraham lived some distance from the leading commercial centers), she nevertheless kept herself looking attractive for her husband.

Some Christian women do not see the need to follow Sarah's example. They have been reared in a tradition that teaches that plainness is a virtue. They misunderstand Peter's teaching that a wife "should not depend *solely* on an elaborate coiffure, or on the wearing of jewelry or fine clothes, but *also* on the inner personality—the unfading loveliness of a calm and gentle spirit . . ." (1 Peter 3:3-4).[1] As a result, when their husbands return home after a day at the office—where their senses have been bombarded by engaging women—they are greeted at the door by someone who bears closer resemblance to the "Wreck of the Hesperus" than the person they married.

ON BOARD SHIP

Gladys lost her husband while she was only in her mid-forties. At first her relatives and friends rallied around her, but eventually she was left alone. Life seemed to have lost its meaning. Her old vivacity disappeared. After two years of dreary monotony she decided that a change was necessary. A vacation, in fact. She wanted to go somewhere and do something that she had never done before.

It was about this time that Gladys saw an ad in the local newspaper. It was for a cruise to Mexico with stops at different ports along the way. She decided to go. All at once her former buoyancy began to return. She began to plan. She knew that they always had a fancy dress party sometime during the cruise and decided ahead of time what she would wear.

The day of the fancy dress party Gladys visited the beauty parlor. In contrast to the other women who were having their hair suitably set for the evening's festivities, Gladys had only one side of her hair coiffured. The other side was left as bedraggled as it was when she had climbed out of the swimming pool. Her one hand was immaculately manicured, but the other was left devoid even of nail polish. Then, just before dinner, she began dressing. Her one leg was clad in an expensive nylon and a beautiful evening shoe, whereas the other had on it an old stocking which slumped around her ankle and a worn-out slipper. And her dress added the finishing touches to her attire: It was a beautiful, full-length evening dress but, onto one side Gladys had stitched half of a shabby, tattered dress that had long since outlived its usefulness. And tacked lightly to the back was a small sign with the words BEFORE MARRIAGE AND AFTER.

Needless to say Gladys won a prize for the most original costume. What she had so graphically (and mischievously) portrayed was what most married couples have become accustomed to.

A woman's appearance, however, is important. It reveals how she feels about herself. It also discloses her attitude toward her husband. Not all women are possessed of natural beauty, but they can make themselves look attractive. Their efforts at outward adornment, however, should be subordinated to the cultivation of the spirit. Sarah maintained this balance, and Peter uses her as an example of what he has been describing. *"This,"* he says, *"was the secret of the beauty of the holy women of ancient times who trusted in God"* (1 Peter 3:5f.).

It was her spiritual dynamic that kept Sarah from developing those inner tensions that ultimately would have had an effect on her outward appearance (comp. Prov. 15:31; 25:23b; Isa. 3:9). It was her spiritual resources that helped her adjust to the ardors of nomadic life. It was her personal reliance on God that grew in strength and discernment so that at last she came to a place in her experience where she knew that God could and would do the impossible (Heb. 11:11-12). *"And you have become, as it were, her true descendants,"* Peter reminds us, *"as long as you too live good lives and do not give way to unreasonable fears"* (1 Peter 3:6).

PROBLEMS GALORE

Sarah shares a great deal in common with modern women. She travelled continuously: down to Egypt and back again to Bethel, off to the Negev, then to Hebron, a trip to Gerar in Philistia, and several stops for water on the way back. It seemed as if she was always on the move. In this respect those who, as part of the national statistic, relocate every five to seven years because their husbands have been transferred, can learn from Sarah's *"gentle and quiet spirit"* how to avoid the tensions which otherwise might disrupt the home.

Sarah's gentle, quiet temperament came as a result of her strong spiritual commitment. She was one of the minority group who possessed a vital, personal belief in the one true God. When all the world was rushing after idols and worshipping other gods, the stalwart and majestic figure of Abraham stood apart. And when he knelt by the side of some rough-hewn altar, there, kneeling by his side, was his wife. She did not receive communication directly from God as did her husband, but readily accepted whatever he related to her (comp. 1 Cor. 14:35). This made her faith all the more remarkable!

In addition to the constant moving, Sarah also lived with a problem she was powerless to correct. She was childless. God had promised Abraham a son. She, of course, expected to be the child's mother. But she was getting along in years. What was wrong? Why didn't God fulfill His word? The seemingly endless waiting could easily have warped her personality and turned her against her husband, or God, or both. Barrenness in the Near East carried with it a social stigma. Those unable to bear children were looked on as being punished for some previous wrong.[2] They were treated with scorn and contempt. Perhaps this was one of the reasons why Abraham continued to say that Sarah was his sister. But being childless deprived Sarah of a sense of fulfillment. Her maternal instincts were not satisfied, and, worst of all, she was unable to give Abraham what he wanted most, a son.

As we study Sarah's life—from the time we are first introduced to her in Genesis 12—let us read it as if for the first time. Let us feel with her as she and Abraham face the trials as well as the joys of their life together. And most important of all, let us find out what made her such a fine wife.

UNCONSCIOUS VULNERABILITY

Sarah's *"gentle and quiet spirit"* is much in evidence when we consider her identification with Abraham in the "changes of profession" he made.* As with many wives, it was probably easy for her to reside in Ur and be looked up to as the wife of Abraham the merchant. They could live in a spacious two- or three-level home, and everything to delight the senses was close at hand. But each move they made took them farther and farther from the crossroads of culture. Now the things Sarah had taken for granted were hard to come by. In the place of costly silks and perfumes there was only the rudest of clothing. And cooking utensils cluttered up her side of the tent.

In a situation like this—one that went on year after year—Sarah could have become a real "grouch." Her complaining

---

*In Genesis 12 Abraham is a wealthy merchant (v. 5). After visiting Egypt he is rich in cattle and other livestock (Gen. 13:2-7).

and bitterness could have made her extremely hard to live with. The biblical record, however, seems to indicate that instead of constantly bemoaning her fate she was a model wife. H. V. Morton writes of her, "Throughout a life of almost continuous travel, she never argued or asked silly questions . . . When she was told to leave her country and journey into a strange land *to help her husband to fulfill his divinely inspired destiny,"* she readily supported him in all he did.[3] She was a true companion of Abraham's new life of obedience to, and fellowship with God. His life became hers. Where he went she went, not as his shadow, but as a strong influence. Her love and loyalty became the source of his strength, and she was blessed by his devotion to her.

DAUGHTERS OF SARAH

We may validly ask, What may modern women learn from Sarah's experience? What practical help can the precedent she set be to the wife who must follow her upward-reaching husband wherever his company sends him? For him a transfer frequently means promotion, but for her it often tallies up to a loss: of friends and neighbors, of church and social activities, and of a certain acceptability in the community. One wife in Detroit found that her accomplishments meant little or nothing in Boston. Her husband moved from assistant manager in Detroit to manager in Boston. He rode the "crest of the wave" and could not understand why his wife appeared chronically depressed. She tried hard to be supportive, but could not make the transition. She felt she "didn't belong" in Boston. Her new neighbors looked down on her because she was "from Detroit." And the social milieu—which had been so much a part of her life before— seemed to be sewed up too tight to permit an "outsider" to enter.

Other wives leave their employment—school, hospital, or company in which they have worked for several years—only to find that a new job is hard to come by, or is at a lower level on the social or income scale. Here again they feel "short-changed" by the move. Their husband's credentials are readily transferable; theirs are not.

When counseling people in situations such as those described above, psychologists attempt to build the "ego strength" of their clients. They try to help them make the necessary emotional adjustments to their new situations. They endeavor to re-establish their identities—the sense of belonging, worth, and competence—that we all need if we are to function efficiently. Sarah, however, lived long before psychologists began offering help and understanding to a growing number of troubled people. How did she manage?

THE POWER WITHIN

From what Peter tells us, Sarah must have accepted all that happened as from the Lord. Actively stated, this meant that she lived in happy submission to the will of God. She was "internally oriented" (Rom. 8:5b; contra. vv. 5a, 6-8).[4] The genuineness of her relationship brought a new awareness of reality into her life. This contributed to her feeling acceptance. She knew that both she and Abraham were part of a new program. God had chosen and called them. In this she felt secure.

Being a part of the outworking of God's purpose also gave Sarah an awareness of her value. She was important to Him. By fulfilling His plan for her life—even in the little things she did—Sarah knew that she was cooperating in a program far beyond her own imagining. And with such confidence she could face the future.

It is this inner dynamic—this feeling of security, worth, and competence (which is as important in a woman as it is in a man)—that helps people adjust to the harsh realities and inequities of life. They can draw strength from their relationship with the Lord, and exert a stabilizing influence on those around them.

With her confidence firmly "anchored" in the Lord, Sarah is able to relate to Abraham from a position of strength. A beautiful spirit of trust and affection exists between them. She exercises authority over the household, and he treats her as his equal. And through the years of waiting for the child of promise to be born, her faith joins with Abraham's as together they rest in expectation on the promise of God.

Abraham's life, however, is filled with variety, and this

helps him through the long period of waiting. He visits his herdsmen in different parts of the Negev, sells sheep and cattle to the Canaanites, deals with the Hittites, makes treaties with the Philistines, forms a military alliance with the Amorites, attacks a coalition of kings from the East, and enjoys variation as well as excitement.[5]

Sarah, however, remains at home. Does she feel neglected? Does she resent being left by herself? Does she show her displeasure in snide little ways that make Abraham feel uneasy and unwanted when he returns? And do these times of loneliness make her feel more acutely her childless state?

It is hard for a wife to be supportive of her husband when his work takes him away from home for weeks on end, or consumes a major portion of his time each evening. This is particularly true of those whose husbands are pastors or politicians, salesmen or students. A wife, in general, is more interested in people—relatives or friends—and less inclined to take an interest in the marketing of a new product, the intricacies of a new contract, a power struggle over a vacancy in the company, or any one of a number of things that are of great importance to her husband. She operates more on an intuitive, feeling level. She thrives when surrounded by a sense of communion, a feeling of closeness, and the spontaneous outpouring of affection. Emotionally, she wants to share meaningfully in the life of her spouse.

PILLOW TALK

It was this desire to share meaningfully in the life of Abraham that led Sarah to suggest that he take Hagar, her servant, as his concubine (Gen. 16:2-4a). It probably happened one evening when the intimacy of their relationship and the satisfaction she felt prompted her to make the suggestion. God had promised Abraham a son (Gen. 12:1-3), and now, after ten years of waiting, Sarah (being seventy-five years old) has passed the time of life when she can expect to have children. She can think of no other way for Abraham to have a son other than through "adoption." In the day in which they live, taking a second wife in order to have children by her is a perfectly natural thing to do. Recent archaeological excavations at Nuzi—a city whose culture parallels that of Abraham and Sarah—have uncovered a marriage contract which throws light on this.

Gilimninu has been given in marriage to Shennima.

If Gilimninu bears (children) Shennima shall not take another wife; but if Gilimninu does not bear, Gilimninu shall acquire a woman of the land of Lullu as wife for Shennima, and Gilimninu may not send the offspring away. Any son that may be born to Shennima of Gilimninu to (these) sons shall be given (all) the land and buildings of every sort. (However), if she does not bear a son, (then) the daughter of Gilimninu shall take one portion of the property. . . .[6]

Abraham follows his wife's suggestion and Hagar's son becomes Sarah's. She now experiences a measure of fulfillment as she begins to rear Ishmael. Unfortunately problems arise with Hagar (Gen. 16:4b). In spite of the tension, Sarah continues to enjoy the love and confidence of her husband. This is obvious, for when she remonstrates with him he replies with gentleness and discretion. His reassurance is sufficient to allay her fears of being replaced in his affections by her maid.

REAFFIRMATION OF A PROMISE

The record in Genesis (17:15-21; 18:9-15) might leave us with the impression that Sarah is only mildly responsive to the Lord and not equal to her husband's faith—supportive of him, yes; but not his counterpart spiritually. This is possible, for real spiritual compatibility is hard to achieve. The writer of Hebrews, however, shows us that Sarah's faith was growing and maturing all the time (Heb. 11:11). In her experience she ultimately reaches the place where she believes God can and will do the impossible. And when this happens, He does.

Let us review the events leading up to the birth of her son, Isaac. In chapter 16, when Sarah is seventy-five years old, she despairs of ever having children herself. To be sure, God has promised Abraham a son, but He had never said she was to be the child's natural mother. She therefore suggests the adoption of her husband's child by a secondary wife or concubine.

About fourteen years later, after Ishmael has been born and everything seems to be working out as planned, God appears to Abraham. His words are startling. *"As for Sarah your wife . . . I will bless her, and indeed I will give you a son by her."*

All of this comes as a surprise to Abraham, and he questions inwardly *"Will a child be born to a man one hundred years old? And will Sarah, who is ninety years old, bear a child?"* (Gen. 17:15-17). Then, concluding that the whole matter is preposterous, he offers God a more plausible solution. *"Oh that Ishmael might live before you"* (Gen. 17:18). In other words, "Lord, let Your promise be fulfilled in Ishmael."

It is at this juncture that God becomes emphatic. *"No, but Sarah your wife shall bear you a son, and you shall call his name Isaac"* (Gen. 17:19).

Now imagine what happens when Abraham informs Sarah of this conversation. Her response is one of unbelief. Perhaps for this reason—and because she is to play such a vital part in God's redemptive program—God appears in a different way a short time later (Gen. 18:1-5). On this occasion the "Guests" Abraham is entertaining ask about Sarah. Verse 13 identifies the Visitors. Then God says, *"I will surely return to you at this time next year; and behold, Sarah your wife will have a son."*

Sarah, of course, is listening behind the partition of the tent (Gen. 18:9) and she laughs inwardly at the thought. *"The LORD says to Abraham, 'Why did Sarah laugh, saying, "Shall I indeed bear now that I am so old?" Is anything too difficult for the LORD? At the appointed time I shall return to you, at this time next year, and Sarah shall have a son.' "*

In this personal encounter with God, Sarah's faith revives. However, now it is a different kind of confidence that she possesses. Previously she had been a sharer in Abraham's belief; she had believed the promise God had made to him. Now she has a personal reliance of her own. And she finds God to be as good as His word, for she conceives and bears a son to Abraham *"at the appointed time of which God had spoken"* (Gen. 21:1-2). And Abraham calls his son's name Isaac.

Sarah, of course, is not without her faults. At the weaning of Isaac her anger blazes out against Ishmael. True to life, she becomes a mother fighting for the rights of her own child (Gen. 21:8-12). She lives to be one hundred and twenty-seven, and is the only woman in the Bible whose age at the time of death is given. The reason seems to be that we might know of her thirty-seven years of happy enjoyment of her son. God's blessings were not curtailed or diminished on account of her long wait for them.

APPROACHING THE IDEAL

It is as a wife that Sarah makes an indelible impression on us. Her loyalty to and identification with her husband is truly commendable. The Scripture presents her as the kind of wife who encouraged him at great cost to herself. And the hardships she faced served to bring her faith to maturity. Ultimately she was tested regarding a physical impossibility and found God to be the One who could do the impossible. She then received the blessing God had promised and lived to enjoy it.

Interaction

1. We are living in a day when it is fashionable to attend seminars for the enrichment of the marriage and the family. Much of what we learn at these meetings is helpful. Often, however, there is a neglected element; one which Peter alluded to when, after speaking of Sarah, he said, "And you have become, as it were, her true descendants as long as you *do* what is right" (1 Peter 3:6). What is important to God is not so much the new truths we learn, but the practicing of what we already know. Engage in some introspection. What have been some of the points of tension in your relationship lately? How were they resolved? Could things have been handled differently in the light of this verse?

2. According to a national survey each family can expect to move at least once every seven years. What may wives do to make this a family affair? How may they help (i.e., be creatively supportive of) their husbands? In what ways can they best involve their children?

3. Explore the ways in which the vibrancy and reality of one's spiritual experience can contribute to a "gentle and quiet spirit." What substitutes are we most prone to offer in place of the real thing? How may these be detected? In what ways may they be overcome?

4. Sarah bore a life-long social stigma: she was barren. List some present-day stigmas our culture has foisted on to people. What may husbands (or the Christian community) do to relieve these pressures?

5. The difficulties of life are designed to lead us to maturity (James 1:2-4; 1 Peter 1:6-7, 15; 1 Thess. 4:3). Beginning with Genesis 12:1-4, discuss the progress of Sarah's faith. It would have been easy for her to regard her husband as either a misguided "crusader" (engaged in a spiritual quest for a country in much the same way that medieval knights sought for a country "the Holy Grail") or a deluded "crack-pot" (circumcising himself and others in response in response to some (supposed) revelation). What do we learn from her example? What does it teach us of the *reality* of *her* spiritual experience?

10

THE MARRIAGE MYSTIQUE

Regardless of how careful a man is, his wife always finds
out his failings.

—J. M. Barrie

Genesis 26

In ancient Sparta, marriage to a Spartan girl was compulsory. How these marriages were arranged is uncertain. One theory survives. An equal number of boys and girls was thrust simultaneously into a dark room, and each boy married the girl he caught.[1] This was supposed to be more civilized than the "bride by capture" system that had been practiced before. In a very real sense these young people were called upon to love[2] the one they married (not marry the one they loved).

Among the Hebrews marriages frequently were pre-arranged.[3] A contract was drawn up, sometimes before the children were even born. So rigid were the laws governing this kind of agreement that if the groom died any time before the wedding, his intended bride was spoken of as a widow[4] and had to dress accordingly.

With the advent of modern technology we now have mate selection by computer. Personality tests are given and, on the basis of the responses, cards are prepared. These are then fed into the computer and matched with others bearing compatible characteristics. This might seem like a novel idea but, as one marriage counselor observed, "From time immemorial girls of marriageable age have had mothers who were calculators." One primary problem in this kind of mate selection is that those who set out to marry their ideal, frequently find that the experience turns into an ordeal. More than compatibility is needed if a marriage is to succeed. There needs to be a commitment to one another which includes working through the problems that arise in a relationship.

RETROSPECT AND PROSPECT

How, then, may the choice of a wife be made with fewer of the hazards that seem to blight the marriages of so many? The answer may be found in the familiar story of Isaac and Rebekah. Genesis 24 reads so perfectly that it cannot be improved upon. Here are some of the principles that Christian would-be-weds will do well to follow:

> —Rebekah was chosen from among those of Abraham's relatives who worshipped God and, on that account, had been kept from the moral depravity of idolatry (v. 16). Abraham was anxious to avoid "yoking" Isaac to an unbeliever.
> —Rebekah was the specific object of much prayer (vv. 12, 26, 63).
> —God led in the circumstances surrounding her selection (v. 40), and she was willing to leave her home and marry Isaac (vv. 51, 58).

This took the anxiety out of the situation for both of them. At God's appointed time He brought them together (Gen. 24:61; comp. Gen. 2:22b). Up until then they were free to develop as persons and rest in His all-wise providence. At the right time His will for them became a reality. And God, who is unchanging, can do the same for all who will trust Him. Such confidence relieves us of apprehension over the future, and prevents people from hastening into unwise marriages.

WHO IS COMPATIBLE?

As we examine the personalities first of Isaac and then, in our next chapter, of Rebekah, we will need to see them against the backdrop of their families and their times. The lives of Isaac's father Abraham, and his son Jacob, stand out prominently in the record, but of him much less is said. His life is practically devoid of striking incident; his character is quiet and unobtrusive.[5] He does not appear as an innovator; and yet there is a quality of greatness about him.

The closer we examine the sacred text for a clue to Isaac's greatness, the more contemporary become the problems he faced. The answer to our quest for the secret of his moral and spiritual stature is to be found in the words of Jacob to Laban. At the time they are spoken, Jacob has been away from home for more than twenty years (Gen. 31:41). He had never been particularly close to his father, Isaac, but with the passing of time minor issues have been forgotten, and only the most significant things are recalled to mind. In confronting his father-in-law, Laban, he takes an oath by all that he regards as holy. Because he can think of nothing more impressive, he swears by *"the fear of his father Isaac"* (Gen. 31:53). But what does he mean? Is he afraid of his father? A closer look at the text shows that he is referring, not to dread of a person (i.e., Isaac), but to Isaac's God.

The *"fear of the Lord,"* we are told, *"is the beginning of wisdom"* (Prov. 1:7). This does not mean that God either expects or is honored by a neurotic apprehension on the part of those who call themselves His children. The *"fear of the Lord"* is not a servile, cringing dread, but rather reverence for God. It means standing in awe of Him, and this is the first lesson in the school of heavenly wisdom.

What Jacob implied in his oath to Laban was the solemn realization of who God is, and the finest example of a relationship with God that he could think of was that of his own father.

With this in mind, let us examine some of the events in Isaac's life to see how his God-consciousness became a dynamic force in his experience.

THE GOD OF COMFORT

From infancy, Isaac had been reared in his mother's tent, and when she died he missed her greatly. Sarah had imparted to her son something of her own disposition. Isaac grew to manhood with a gentle, obedient, sensitive temperament which showed itself to the last in his amiable, peaceful, character. Her influence was made all the more venerable by his integrity and devotion to the Lord.[6]

Abraham sensed how much his son suffered after Sarah's death, and when he felt it expedient, he sent Eleazar, his servant, to Paddan-aram ("the fields of Aram"), to seek a wife for his son. Eleazar found Rebekah, a girl in her late teens, and returned with her to Isaac. *"And Isaac brought her into his mother Sarah's tent, and he took Rebekah, and she became his wife; and he loved her; and Isaac was comforted after his mother's death"* (Gen. 24:67).

In all of this we see how, in a most practical way, God undertook to meet Isaac's need, heal his hurt, give him someone to love, and lead him unto a deeper, more meaningful kind of relationship.

THE POWER OF PRAYER

From a consideration of Genesis 25:20, 26 we glean the fact that Isaac and Rebekah live happily in Beersheba (or its neighborhood) for twenty years. God is good to them. There is no need for them to move. The rains come on time and there is always sufficient provender for their animals. Only one thing disturbs the happy tranquility of their home. As with Sarah before her, Rebekah appears to be barren. She feels that her condition may be due to divine disfavor. What had she done that God was withholding children from her (comp. 1 Sam. 1:5)?

In this situation, and without waiting for his wife to goad him into action, Isaac prays to the Lord (Gen. 25:21). God hears his prayer, and Rebekah conceives.

Isaac's example is important. He earnestly intercedes (Heb., *athar,* "to plead") on behalf of his wife. In this we see first, his own relationship with God; and second, his loving concern for Rebekah. His action illustrates the fact that the godly man's prayers are his best biography, his most exact portrait. By means of prayer he releases the energies of God.

Rebekah is encouraged by Isaac's example, and when the children struggle within her, she inquires of the Lord the cause. In answer, she is told:

> *Two nations are in your womb;*
> *And two peoples shall be separated from your*
>   *body;*
> *And one people shall be stronger than the other;*
> *And the older shall serve the younger.*

What God had predicted comes to pass. Twins are born. As the boys grow, the older, Esau, becomes a skillful hunter, a man of the field; while Jacob, the younger, is a peaceful man, living in tents. Isaac, Rebekah's quiet, meditative husband, likes the stalwart, aggressive Esau, for he reminds him of all the qualities he admires most in his wife. Rebekah, on the other hand, likes the reserved, domesticated Jacob. And what parent cannot see in his or her mind's eye, Isaac walking with young Esau and telling him about the wild animals and the wilderness; while Rebekah, with Jacob mixing dough by her side, encourages him as he helps her with the evening meal.

ONE BIG MISTAKE

Apparently all goes well with Isaac and Rebekah until a famine devastates the land. It is so severe that it can only be likened to the one that caused crops to fail and cattle to die nearly a century earlier (Gen. 26:1).[7] In order to protect his flocks and herds, Isaac goes to Gerar in the land of the Philistines.

Being away from the old, familiar homestead, Isaac succumbs to the same fears Abraham experienced (Gen. 12:11-13; 20:2-7). He is nearly seventy-five years old, while Rebekah is little more than fifty. As with Sarah, Rebekah must have retained her youthful appearance, and Isaac feels that the Philistines might kill him and take his wife. When asked about her, he therefore says, *"She is my sister"* (Gen. 26:7).

All goes well for a while until one day Abimelech the king looks out of his window and sees Isaac caressing Rebekah. He summons Isaac to appear before him and exposes his deception (Gen. 26:8-11). He then issues a decree, *"He who touches this man or his wife shall surely be put to death."*

DEVISIVE REACTION

Imagine Rebekah's reaction when she learns, perhaps while shopping in the city, of what Isaac has done. There is embarrassment over being seen in an intimate situation by Abimelech, and anger that her husband should institute a plan for his preservation without considering or consulting her. Anger turns to resentment and, not being of the temperament to forgive, she nurses a grievance and invests more and more of her time in her favorite son, Jacob. Never again in Scripture do we read of Rebekah saying a kind word to, or doing a kind deed for, her husband.

Anger is very destructive of our relationships. If not handled properly it will cause more and more dissension. In marriage it often results in frigidity in women and impotency in men.

Isaac, of course, has been soundly rebuked by Abimelech. A man as sensitive as he, must have been chagrined at such a reprimand. He realizes his mistake and reverts back to his former confidence in the Lord.[8] His lapse in faith has been temporary and he quickly recovers. But something has gone out of his marriage. He feels himself rejected by his wife[9] In spite of her flinty intransigence, he never wavers in his devotion to her, nor does he take concubines into his tent to satisfy his physical needs (comp. Gen. 25:6). Instead, he moves outside the city and begins to raise crops. And God blesses him (Gen. 26:12).

FURTHER INJUSTICE

It is as a consequence of God's lovingkindness to him that Isaac is called upon to face another test. This time from the Philistines. They envy his prosperity and thrust him out from among them (Gen. 26:16). They also appropriate the crops he has labored to cultivate.

Realizing that he has no claim to the land, Isaac leaves. There is no exchange of words and no bitter remonstrance. His confidence is in God's sovereignty and Jacob, seeing it, is impressed by his father's meek (not weak!) attitude.

Isaac and his household settle in a wadi between Gerar and Beersheba. There his herdsmen dig a well. It is hard, backbreaking work. When they find water it is only to have the herdsmen of Gerar dispute with them over it (Gen. 26:19-20). Again they move, and again they dig a well. Again they find water, and again the Philistines quarrel with them (Gen. 26:21). They have no alternative but to move once more. This time they dig a well and there is no dispute (Gen. 26:22).

In all of this we see Isaac's gentle and amiable disposition. He is a lover of peace.

But isn't Isaac too passive? Couldn't he have learned something from modern psychologists who conduct workshops and hold seminars on assertion training?

In time Abimelech, king of Gerar, leaves Philistia and comes to visit Isaac in Beersheba. Listen to Isaac as he speaks:

> *Why have you come to me, since you hate me, and have sent me away from you* (Gen. 26:27)?

Here is a perfect assertive statement. Isaac's "why" question has the effect of placing Abimelech on the defensive.[10] There is also a clear reminder (but in a few words!) of the wrong done to him. There is no "name-calling," but only a manly expression of his hurt.

Abimelech's response is tactful. He turns aside the thrust of Isaac's question and commends his host for what to him is most evident—*his spiritual commitment* and the evidence of God's blessing on his life.

> *We see plainly that the LORD has been with you; so we said, "Let there now be an oath between us . . ."* (Gen. 26:28).

So Isaac's discretion, in not retaliating to the injustice done him in Gerar, works to his advantage in Beersheba. And Jacob again sees the effect of his father's quiet, persistent confidence in the Lord.

SHUNTED ASIDE

Time passes. Isaac is old. His vision is blurred. Rebekah is no comfort to him. The days are long and filled with the monotonous sameness that old people dread. Only Esau visits his blind father and, to make these visits memorable, he brings with him some venison such as his father loves.

Perhaps during a period of illness, Isaac feels that his end is near. Now is the time for him to bestow his blessings on his sons. By right of primogeniture the first-born should receive a double portion of his father's estate and, in patriarchal times, become not only the head of the family or tribe, but act as their spiritual leader as well.[11]

Rebekah overhears Isaac speaking to Esau:

Behold now, I am old and I do not know the day of my death. Now then, I pray you, please take your hunting gear, your quiver and your bow, and go into the field and hunt game for me; and prepare a savory dish for me such as I love, and bring it to me that I may eat, so that my soul may bless you before I die (Gen. 27:2-4).

The story is filled with pathos. The blind old man, believes himself to be on his deathbed. His sole comfort is a son who, as with himself, has been ostracized by the one who as wife and mother, should have been a unifying force in the home.

The story of Rebekah's deception is well known. She prepares a meal for Isaac and sends Jacob in to obtain the blessing intended for Esau (Gen. 27:6-29). Her plan succeeds, and yet she fails. Isaac is duped by her chicanery. He blesses Jacob, but when Esau finds out that he has been cheated (Gen. 27:30-41) he vows to kill his brother. To save Jacob's life, Rebekah devises another plan. She complains bitterly to Isaac about Esau's wives and concludes, *"I am tired of living because of the daughters of Heth; if Jacob should take a wife . . . from the daughters of the land, what good will my life be to me"* (Gen. 27:46).

Notice the emphasis on *"I . . . my . . . me."* Rebekah is preoccupied with herself, not Isaac. Even Jacob, her dearest, takes second place. There is no indication in what she says of God or of doing His will. All she does is manipulate Isaac into sending Jacob away, so that he can be saved from Esau.

Isaac, guileless as usual, agrees with Rebekah's proposal and Jacob is sent north to Paddan-aram. Their marriage, however, which had begun so well has lost its mystique. Neither Isaac nor Rebekah find joy in their relationship. Isaac remains loyal to Rebekah because of his reverence for (i.e., fear of) God. And Rebekah stays with Isaac because it is convenient. But instead of dying as Rebekah expects (Gen. 27:25c) Isaac lives on for thirty or more years and dies at the age of one hundred and eighty (Gen. 35:27-29). Rebekah predeceases him and never sees her favorite son again (contra. Gen. 27:44-45).

NEW VALUES

As we *review* Isaac's life we find him to be gentle and amiable to the end. He was the kind of person many a woman would give all she possessed to have as a husband. He loved his wife Rebekah with unquenchable devotion. Even after long years of marriage, their love was spontaneous and exhilarating. Only once did he stumble, and for this his wife never forgave him.

As a father, Isaac was not wholly free from blemish, since he allowed himself a favorite son. But even to Jacob, the son whom he loved least, he was gentle and forgiving (Gen. 28: 1-4).

As a farmer, he passed a quiet, patient, unadventurous life in the Negev. His gracious behavior was much in evidence and after being thrust out of Philistia, he nevertheless entertained Abimelech and his retinue; and they felt sufficiently at home with him to spend the night in his tent. He did not return evil for evil or insult for insult, but imparted blessing instead (1 Peter 3:9).

And when he realized how wrong he had been to think that the blessing of God could be given to Esau, he quickly repented of his act (Gen. 27:33).

In the final analysis, it was the vitality of his faith—that which Jacob referred to as *"the fear* (i.e., reverence for God) *of his father Isaac"*—that kept him from becoming (a) bitter when rebuked by Abimelech, (b) vengeful when deprived of water rights by the herdsmen of Gerar, (c) cynical when scorned by his wife, and (d) morose when faced with years of blindness and loneliness. And it is our relationship with the Lord that will help us overcome the vicissitudes of life and make the greatest impact on our children.

Interaction

1. Describe the influence of Sarah on her son, Isaac. What do you consider to be the most significant feature?
2. In what ways do you think Isaac and Rebekah's personalities complemented (i.e., added to each other to make them complete) during the first twenty years of their marriage?

3. Why is favoritism of one child by a parent detrimental to the growth of all the children?
4. What is there in the conversations between Isaac and Abimelech that is of value to us in our interpersonal relationships (Gen. 26:9-10, 26-31)? Is there any evidence that he forgave Abimelech for the wrong done to him?
5. Of what practical value was Isaac's God-centered life when he faced (a) famine, (b) rejection by the Philistines, (c) ostracism by his wife, and (d) the loneliness and dependence of his old age?

11

THE MIDDLESCENT MALAISE

Marriages work best where trust is honored, where views are shared, where companionship is treasured, and where love is given a chance to flow freely.
—C. Neil Strait

Genesis 24 and 27

Little Lucy was learning to read. One afternoon she came running home from school and excitedly told her mother the story she had read that day.

"There was a very beautiful girl named Snow White. And she lived in a little house in the woods with seven little men. And one day a wicked witch gave her a shiny apple. But Snow White didn't know that it was poisoned. And when she took a bite of the apple she fell asleep. And then a prince came riding up to the cottage on his horse. And he kissed her and she woke up."

"And Mommy, then guess what happened."

"They lived happily ever after."

"No, no, no!" protested Lucy, "they got married."

SYMBOLIC SIGNS

How true! Marriage does not always measure up to the expectations of the couple. Wedlock can become deadlock. Tensions can develop. The couple can drift apart. They may share the same address, but loving communication has disappeared from their relationship.

But what causes the buck-passing, the blaming, the fault-finding or the jockeying for position in the marriage-go-round?

When we analyze the situation—which, unfortunately, is painfully prevalent in cases where couples have been married for ten years or more—we find that both parties have contributed to the breakdown of their marriage. Patterns of behavior have developed. They can now predict each others' responses to different situations. They may long for closeness, intimacy, and companionship, but due to their well established behavioral "grooves," they sabotage each others' attempts to break down the barriers that separate them. As a result, they end up living separate lives even though they remain under the same roof.

The tragedy of such a relationship may be traced primarily to neglect. The couple have not given each other the reciprocal love and attention each one needs.[1] Loneliness, a feeling of isolation, and discouragement are the eventual result.

To regain the lost intimacy there must be a determined effort on the part of both husband and wife to deal lovingly with their problems. And there must be forgiveness for past wrongs—of omission as well as commission—before the healing of their marriage can take place. These healing roles go against the grain of our natural reactions. How then are we to do what comes *un*naturally?

Fortunately for us, all of this is illustrated for us in the marriage of Rebekah and Isaac. Their problems, arising after twenty years of marriage, demonstrate the kinds of tensions which can bring on "middlescent malaise." They also act as "guideposts" for us so that we can learn from their experience.

FINE BEGINNING

When Eleazar, Abraham's servant, is sent north to the home of Laban in Paddan-aram, he prays that God will guide him to the girl of His choice. He also asks for a sign.

> *O LORD, the God of my master Abraham, please grant me success today, and show lovingkindness to my master Abraham. Behold, I am standing by the spring, and the daughters of the men of the city are coming out to draw water. Now, may it be that the girl to whom I shall say, "Please let down your jar so that I may drink," and who answers, "Drink,*

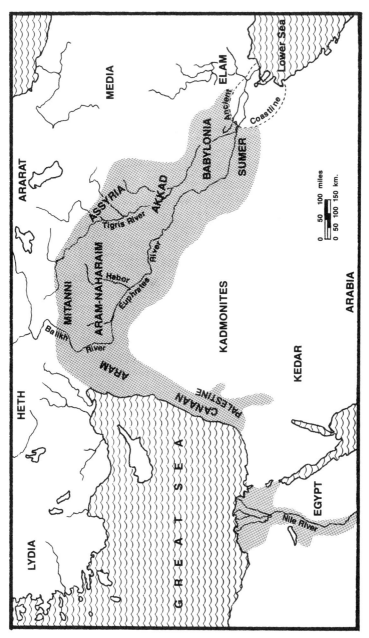

The Fertile Crescent

*and I will water your camels also;" may she be the
one whom You have appointed for your servant
Isaac* (Gen. 24:12-14).

As Eleazar finishes his prayer, he sees a very beautiful
young girl approaching the well. He asks her for a drink, and
she responds by offering to water his camels as well.* She is
polite, well poised, gracious and generous. Eleazar is
impressed by her vivacious, kindly manner. She is in every
way an ideal young woman and a suitable bride for Isaac.
And the biblical writer adds, she is *"a virgin, and no man has
had sexual relations with her"* (Gen. 24:16).

When Rebekah has finished watering the camels, Eleazar
presents her with engagement presents: a gold ring and two
gold bracelets (Gen. 24:22).[2] Such impressive gifts would
cause any young girl's heart to beat faster. She leaves
Abraham's servant by the well and hastens to her brother's
home to tell her mother. They then entertain Eleazar for the
night, and in the morning, Rebekah leaves with him to go
meet her husband (Gen. 24:54-60).

It is a long journey, and en route, they pass through
Damascus, skirt the highlands of Lebanon with snowcapped
Mt. Hermon, traverse the green hills of Galilee, and finally
draw near to the yellow plains and sandy dunes of Beersheba.
As they approach the encampment of Abraham, Rebekah sees
a young man walking towards them. *"Who is that man walking
in the field?"* she asks. When she is told that it is Isaac, she
dismounts from her camel and veils herself (Gen. 24:64-65).
The former act shows her graciousness and discretion, while
the latter is indicative of her modesty and sense of propriety.

It is possible that Isaac gave a feast that night to honor the
safe arrival of his wife. No other ceremony was necessary.
Then he *"brought her into his mother Sarah's tent, and he
took Rebekah, and she became his wife."*

As a couple they have everything in their favor. Isaac is
tender and affectionate; Rebekah is warm and responsive. If

---

*To draw water from a well to slake the thirst of Eleazar's camels (Gen. 24:10) was
no light task, for each camel could easily drink ten gallons of water.

ever a marriage was "made in heaven"—as the saying goes— theirs was. They can now "live happily ever after." Certainly this is what we would like to believe.

DEVELOPING LIFESTYLE

In his book *To Understand Each Other,*[3] the renowned Swiss physician, Dr. Paul Tournier, discusses how proper communication can be attained and maintained in marriage. His observation of marriages over the years has led him to conclude that most marriages pass through stages. Those which begin with a real commitment on the part of the couple can survive the adjustments that must be made in the first twelve months. He then analyzes the developing relationships in five-year periods.

The first five years are ones of growing intimacy. The couple feels that they understand each other. They share similar tastes (in foods, furniture, friends) and interests (hobbies, entertainment, church). They are also concerned for each other and readily sense each other's wishes and feelings.

The second phase normally covers the fifth to tenth years. In this stage each partner begins to realize that the other is not as similar to themselves as they once thought. Faults previously overlooked begin to surface. Outside interests, the pressures of "getting ahead," and a score of distractions begin to make their presence felt. Now a wife (or husband) will complain, "But I cannot understand him (or her). . . ." And with this comes the temptation to withdraw from one another and find fulfillment and satisfaction in doing other things.

Between the tenth and fifteenth years of marriage the relationship between husband and wife undergoes a severe strain. It develops in accordance with the direction taken in the preceding five years. One personality begins to dominate the relationship, the struggle for happiness is relinquished, and resentment, bitterness and rebellion bring about frequent disputes that are never settled.

Often a couple stay together solely for the sake of their children, or because their parents or church-going friends would frown on them for getting a divorce.

In the case of Isaac and Rebekah their relationship did not deteriorate as rapidly. Their social structure was different and the pace of life was slower. Rebekah, however, did emerge as the dominant personality.

As we take up the story once more, let's look for those principles which will help us avoid the "middlescent malaise."

TURNING POINT

Through twenty years of marriage, Rebekah remains childless. Her condition seems to be contrary to the purpose of God (Gen. 17:19, 21; 22:16-18). Concern over her situation and a little anxiety would be natural. She may also have feared that Isaac might take a second wife in order to assure himself of an heir.[4]

Instead of doing what was customary in the ancient Near East in those days, Isaac intercedes for his wife. God hears his prayer and Rebekah conceives. Twin boys are born and she feels doubly blessed. After such a long wait she now experiences the fulfillment of her maternal instincts. She is mindful of the Lord's words that her *"elder son* (Esau) *will serve the younger* (Jacob)," and openly favors Jacob. Her husband is much older than she, and should he predecease her, she will naturally be dependent on her children. And who better to spend her declining days with than the easy-going Jacob. How little she realizes that *children are temporary, marriage is permanent.*

SYMBOLIC SIGNS

The arrival of the twins seems to have been the beginning of a division in Isaac and Rebekah's relationship. The fact that each parent favored one of the boys seems indicative of a subtle "parting of the ways." They each become child-centered. To be sure Rebekah has emerged as the dominant personality in the home, but this does not automatically signal strife. Open communication between them could easily have eased the tensions that were bound to develop.

It is the ability to communicate with one another that becomes increasingly difficult with the passing of time. Initially a couple's feelings may be amoral.[5] They may be neither good nor bad. Only if these feelings are left unexpressed and unresolved do they begin to fester. When this happens they poison the relationship.

In instituting a plan of open, honest, loving communication, the couple should studiously avoid implying by their words any judgment of the other person. If the other person feels "put down," he (or she) also feels the need to justify himself (or herself) in order to preserve his (or her) fragile sense of esteem.

Second, a person's feelings must be integrated with the intellect and the will. Unchecked by the rational thought processes of the mind, or denied expression through an enlightened will, one's emotions may result in punitive measures to avenge a wrong, or the repression of a hurt because confrontation is threatening.

Third, the candid expression of the way we feel, honestly reported (but without recrimination) and equally as honestly heard by our empathetic spouse, is the only way to keep the lines of communication open.

The counsel of the apostle Paul is also vitally important if proper communication is to be maintained. He said, "In your anger, do not sin. Do not let the sun set while you are still angry" (Eph. 4:26). In other words, let your feelings of hurt or resentment be known to the person who has offended you as soon as possible. In this way you are able to seek an early reconciliation—not on the basis of compromise, but out of mutual love and respect—and the devil will be prevented from using the occasion to lead you into sin (Eph. 4:27).

THE COMMUNICATION GAP

When Isaac and Rebekah go to Gerar it becomes evident that their relationship is not as close as it had once been. On being asked about Rebekah, Isaac says, *"She is my sister."*

In fairness to Isaac, it should be said that with his temperament he was not likely to be the one who would harbor grudges against Rebekah. On this occasion he was overawed by the Philistines, and the consistency of his walk before the Lord was momentarily interrupted. This does not mean that Rebekah was solely responsible for the rupture in their relationship. In all probability they had gradually drifted apart and slowly became aware of the fact that they were not as close as formerly. This would be particularly true whenever they had differences of opinion over how to rear their children.

It often happens that couples who drift apart have mini-reconciliations. It may have been on one of these occasions—with Rebekah feeling very benign—that Abimelech observed them in an intimate situation (Gen. 26:8). If this was so, then imagine Rebekah's feelings when she learned a day or two later that Isaac had denied being her husband. It would be quite natural for her to feel hurt and to express her resentment in some way. We do not know what took place in their tent that night, but we do know that from that time onwards Isaac was the object of her scorn.

THE INTIMATE ENEMY

Without presuming to be judgmental, it may be said that while feelings of hurt and resentment arise in any marriage, there is a "more excellent way" to handle them (1 Cor. 12:31b—13:13) than the one chosen by Rebekah.

1. Instead of retreating from the problem, try loving confrontation. Mistakes are common to sinful human beings—husbands and wives alike. Perhaps there has been wrong on both sides. Self-justification will not help the situation.
2. Try listening to what your spouse is saying. Aim at mutual understanding. Be frank with one another—but avoid harsh, critical comments. Explore the origin of the problem. Be ready to admit your mistake(s).
3. Be quick to forgive. Remember that the Lord Jesus said, "If you forgive men when they sin against you, your heavenly Father will also forgive you. But if you do not forgive men their sins, your Father will not forgive your sins" (Matt. 6:14-15).
4. Remember the covenant you made with one another (Mal. 2:14). It is an earthly counterpart of the spiritual relationship which exists between Christ and His Church (Eph. 5:22-33). He does not expect perfection from us, but works within us to produce the growth (i.e., sanctification or Christ-likeness) He desires. His love for us is such that He freely forgives our sins when we confess them. It is this quality of forgiveness which the Lord Jesus emphasized during his earthly ministry (Matt. 18:21-22, and 23-35), and which Paul (1 Cor. 13:4-13)[6] and John (1 John 1:9) refer to in their letters.

THE DARK SIDE OF LIFE

It is evident from our story that Rebekah withdraws from Isaac. He remains loyal to her, but the joy of their relationship, and the happiness they had once known, has gone. She becomes a self-centered, scheming woman. Jacob replaces his father in her affections, but even he is denied access into the inner sanctum of her heart.

As the years go by, Esau, sensing the need for a woman's love, marries (Gen. 26:34-35). However, he lacks spiritual sensitivity and his Hittite wives are a source of *"bitterness of spirit to Isaac and Rebekah."* They also further alienate him from his mother.

When Isaac begins to lose his sight and then falls ill, both he and Rebekah feel the end is near (Gen. 27:1-2, 45c). He decides to give his paternal blessing to Esau, the only member of his family who has gladdened his declining days.

As we found in our previous chapter, Rebekah is eavesdropping at the curtain of the tent (Gen. 27:5) and hastily devises a strategy to deceive her husband. She successfully substitutes Jacob for Esau (Gen. 27:8-29), and Jacob receives the blessing of the firstborn.

Rebekah's scheme, however, contains a fatal flaw. Esau is so incensed over what has happened that he plans to murder Jacob as soon as Isaac passes away. To save her son, Rebekah devises another plan: She will send Jacob to her brother, Laban, and let him obtain a wife from her people (Gen. 28:1-2).[7] So Jacob is sent away for *"a few days . . . until Esau's anger against you subsides"* (Gen. 27:44-45), but he stays in Paddan-aram for twenty-one years, and Rebekah never sees him again. Her declining days are spent in isolation and loneliness—the frequent experience of those whose conniving, manipulative ways have estranged those nearest and dearest to them.

THE DIVINE PLAN

The Bible reveals the divine pattern for the home. It is clearly described by more than one biblical writer. Paul deals with it at length in Ephesians 5:22—6:2. The family is the "laboratory" in which God enables us to achieve maximum growth and be our greatest blessing. But relationships within the home must be maintained as He intended. If those within the home—husband/wife, parents/children—function as He designed, then the home becomes a "heaven on earth." Where they do not, the reverse is often true.

Unfortunately, as in the case of Rebekah, those within the family circle often play destructive "games," operate in a self-centered way, and call forth the worst in others. In Rebekah's case it was her self-centeredness that lay in the way of her forgiving Isaac the wrong he had done her.

For genuine happiness to result from a marriage, the husband and his wife must complement each other. This is the way Isaac and Rebekah had begun their relationship. She shared meaningfully in his life, and he was happy having someone to love and care for. But when his cowardice was exposed, she seems to have begun trying to subjugate him. This struck at the heart of his masculinity. He did not respond with hostility, but having been rejected by her, he contented himself with other pursuits (Gen. 26:12-22).

How different the outcome can be in *our* relationships if we will practice . . .

—Honest communication without a harsh, judgmental exchange of words.
—Integrate our emotional reactions with our minds and our wills.
—Make our spouse aware of how we feel as a result of what has happened.
—Engage in this loving, honest confrontation at the time we feel upset rather than put it off.
—And be ready to forgive.

Interaction

Open your Bibles to 1 Corinthians 13:4-13. Discuss the ways in which this passage sheds light on (a) the problems of Isaac and Rebekah, and (b) the five points with which this chapter closed. In what specific ways will the practice of the teaching of these verses enrich your marital relationship?

12

YES, THERE'S HOPE

Man seeks his own good at the whole world's cost.
—Robert Browning

Not a deed would he do, nor a word would he utter, 'Till he had weighed its relations to plain bread and butter.
—J. R. Lowell

Genesis 27:1-20, 27; 29:13-25

"All mankind loves a lover," and there is something about the story of Jacob meeting Rachel by the well outside Haran that strikes a romantic chord in our hearts (Gen. 29:1-12). As with young men before and since, Jacob feels that he must do something to impress the beautiful, young Rachel. He, therefore, steps up to the well, and with a display of physical strength, removes the huge stone which lies across it. Then he waters Rachel's sheep.

When Jacob has finished this task the other shepherds take their turn. With their attention thus diverted, Jacob takes Rachel in his arms and kisses her. For him it is love at first sight.

TWO IS ONE TOO MANY

When Laban hears that his sister's son has come courting he remembers the former visit of Eleazar and the expensive gifts Abraham's servant brought. He runs to where Jacob is waiting and invites him into his home.

Jacob, of course, had left Beersheba hurriedly (Gen. 27:41-45) and he hadn't brought any gifts with him. Because he cannot give Laban a suitable *mohar* or dowry for Rachel[1] he agrees to work for him for seven years. ***"So Jacob served*** *seven years for Rachel and they seemed to him but a few days because of his love for her."*

Jacob and Pygmalion shared something in common. They were concerned solely with externals, and Jacob gives no evidence of even considering the spiritual realities which were so important to his father Isaac and his grandfather Abraham.

At the end of seven years when Jacob asks Laban for his wife, Laban makes all the preparations for the celebrations. After the feast, however, when Jacob expects Rachel to be brought heavily veiled to the room where he is waiting, a switch is made. Leah is substituted for her sister (Gen. 29:21-23). With only a small candle lighting the room he does not discover what has happened until the next morning.

But why didn't Jacob refuse to be married to Leah?

Jacob's own guilty conscience may have reminded him of the way in which he had deceived his own father and brother. He was in the kind of situation about which the apostle Paul wrote: *"Do not be deceived: God cannot be mocked. A man reaps what he sows"* (Gal. 6:7).

The same is true of us. God has no favorites. If we wander from the path of His choosing, if we fall into sin, He disciplines us. This may be by allowing the consequences of our misdeeds to catch up with us (Num. 32:23; 1 Tim. 5:24-25). Or it may come through our children.

A few years ago we met an attorney from the East Coast. He had graduated from an "Ivy League" university, and after marrying, began to make a name for himself as a legal counselor. In time he sent his son, Steve Jr., to his *alma mater* with every intention of having him join the firm of which he was now the senior partner.

It wasn't long before news of Steve's misdeeds began to reach him. He decided to visit him. One Friday afternoon he left his office early and drove to the town in which the university was situated. The next morning he met Steve for breakfast. After exchanging the usual pleasantries, he said:

"Steve, is it true that . . ." and he began listing the reports of misconduct he had been receiving.

Steve looked surprised. "Why, y-y-y-es," he stammered, somewhat perplexed.

"Steve, you're ruining your future. You have the opportunity to carve out a fine career for yourself. I want you to join me in the practice. But these reports could ruin your prospects. You are 'mortgaging' your future legal credibility by your present irresponsibility."

Imagine this father's surprise when his son responded, "But Dad, they tell me you did the same things when you were a student."

For Steve's father this was retribution in kind. All of a sudden he remembered as clearly as if it were yesterday his father's remonstrance and his own nonchalance.

DOMESTIC DISCORD

And retribution is the discipline God uses to shape Jacob's character. Dissension plagues his home. It is a "replay" of the tension which existed between Esau and himself. In this particular instance, however, the people involved are his wives. Each one longs for what the other possesses. Leah has children, but lacks her husband's love; and Rachel possesses Jacob's love, but is unable to have children. Their home is one of discord and Jacob, as with Isaac before him, must constantly try to make peace between them.

Social psychologists have divided families into three basic kinds: child-oriented, home-oriented, and parent-oriented. Of these three, Jacob's was the most detrimental to growing children.

In a *child-oriented* home, both parents structure their family around the needs and demands of the children. The husband-wife roles are clearly defined, economic security is highly valued, and community participation is regarded as being very important.

The *home-oriented* model is one in which both parents concentrate on developing congenial interpersonal relationships. In this kind of situation the husband-wife roles tend to overlap, family togetherness is stressed, and community participation is of little importance. This is the ideal, and when strengthened by a strong spiritual commitment, makes a healthy environment for all concerned.

The *parent-oriented* home is one in which the husband and wife concentrate on getting ahead. They are career-oriented, and the family life is built around achievement, personal development, and the acquisition of social skills.[2]

There can be no doubt that the home of Jacob was parent-oriented. His wives were only interested in meeting their individual needs, and Jacob was only interested in getting ahead. As the late W. H. Griffith Thomas so aptly observed, "Where the home life is not full of love and peace, there can be no true witness for God or helpfulness of one another."[3] The spiritual principles which Abraham and Sarah had taken such pains to cultivate in Isaac had been largely lost due to Rebekah's influence on Jacob. And now that Jacob has established a home of his own, these spiritual ideals are totally wanting in his children.[4]

Earlier in his life, Jacob had wanted the "birthright" which fell to the eldest son. Part of the rights of the firstborn was the privilege of serving as the spiritual head of the family (these were in the days before Moses instituted the priesthood)—of representing the family to God, and being God's representative to the family.

Jacob had coveted the prestige which went along with the privilege of possessing the birthright. But in exercising the responsibility which was now his, he shows himself to be sadly deficient.

The same principle holds true in many homes today. Fathers may abdicate their position of leadership in the home and leave their spiritual responsibilities to their wives. It is no wonder that as children grow older they begin to think of family devotions and Bible reading as "kid's stuff," for the men they have observed have stood aloof from it.

It is the solemn responsibility of each father to be God's representative to his home. While all family members should be encouraged to read their Bibles and pray, he is the one commissioned by God to lead the family in a time of meaningful Bible study, and intercede on their behalf.

TURNING POINT

After about seven years of marriage, *"God remembers Rachel"* and she conceives. The birth of her son, Joseph, heralds a turning point in Jacob's life. His thoughts turn homeward. When he makes his intentions known to his father-in-law, Laban persuades him to stay in Haran and set his own wages. Jacob agrees. His distrust of Laban, however, is matched by Laban's distrust of him (Gen. 29:34-35), and Jacob's brothers-in-law keep a watchful eye on him. Equal to the occasion, Jacob develops a strategy of his own (Gen. 29:37-43). The greater his success, the greater becomes their resentment. Finally, the Lord commands him to return to Canaan (Gen. 31:3), and he and his wives leave Haran without Laban's knowledge.[5]

Jacob's heart is far from God, but now that he is obedient to God's general will, he finds his way marked by evidence of God's loving care and provision (comp. Gen. 32:1-2). Confident of God's protection, he sends a message to Esau. His faith receives a severe setback when he hears that his brother is coming to meet him with four hundred armed men (Gen. 32:6, 7). He soon recovers his balance, however, but instead of relying on the Lord, begins his characteristic planning. His intent is to placate Esau with gifts and in this way manipulate him into sparing his life (Gen. 32:20).

As evening falls, Jacob sends his family across the River Jabbok, while he remains on the farther side. As is well known, a man wrestles with him all that night. When day is breaking the stranger blesses him and says, *"Your name shall no longer be Jacob, but Israel* ("prince with God"), *for you have striven with God and with me and have prevailed."*

We might expect that from this time onward Jacob would live up to his new name. Such is not the case (see Gen. 35:10 where God has to repeat the change). Jacob's character does not alter for several years. Evidence of this is to be found in his meeting with Esau. He attempts to "buy" him, feigns submission, and promises to visit him at Mt. Seir, but journeys on to Succoth instead (Gen. 33:12-17). He is still a deceiver ("Supplanter") in spite of his recent spiritual experience.

DANGERS OF COMFORT

We do not know how long Jacob stays at Succoth. When next we read of him he has moved to Shechem (Gen. 33:18).

He *buys* land from the local residents and settles down (Heb. *"he pitches his tent before the city"*). God has promised to give him the land (Gen. 28:13-14), but he cannot trust the Lord and wait for the promise to be fulfilled. God has also told him to *"return to . . . his relatives"* (Gen. 31:3), so his stop in Succoth and stay near Shechem is a plain violation of this command.

To compensate for his disobedience, Jacob builds an altar. However, "worldliness on weekdays is not overcome by early communion on Sunday." Building an altar may ease his guilty conscience, but it will not remove the dangers that threaten his family. Jacob's *only* daughter, Dinah, who has barely entered her teens, goes to find some other girls with whom she can fellowship (Gen. 34:1-3). Instead of finding girls from the village, Shechem, the son of Hamor, finds her. Apparently, in their society, any young woman who is seen unattended is fair "game" for whoever finds her. When Shechem meets with Dinah, he rapes ("defiles")[6] her.

Dinah's brothers are furious over what has happened, and when the men of Shechem propose an alliance (Gen. 34:9-10), they answer them with deceit. They pretend to agree to their proposal, but lay down one condition: the men of Shechem must submit to circumcision. Their plot is a combination of carnality, craft, and cruelty. On the third day, when the men are in pain, Simeon and Levi enter the city and kill every male within its walls.

When we pause to remember that circumcision was a special sign between God and those who recognize His right to rule over them, then the circumcision of the Canaanites in Shechem becomes not only an unprincipled act, but an irreligious one as well. And from whom did they learn such deceit and malice? The answer is twofold: from their father, and from the constant displays of malignity of their mothers.

But what is Jacob's response to the action of his sons? Note his emphasis in Genesis 34:30. *"You . . . me . . . my . . . me . . . I . . . my."* It is reminiscent of his mother (Gen. 27:46). He is completely self-centered! Through their action, his dreams of prosperity have vanished. His presence in the land is resented. His reputation has been ruined (contra. Gen. 26:26-31).

WHERE YOU LIVE DOES MATTER

In our highly mobile society, where we move often, the location of our homes and the place where we rear our children is vitally important. So often decisions as to where to live are made on the basis of a "good" neighborhood where our sons and daughters can mix freely with the "best people," and where social functions and recreational opportunities are readily available.

And all of this is quite legitimate. But has it ever occurred to us when choosing a new neighborhood to inquire into the spiritual climate of the place, what sort of church it has, whether or not the Gospel is preached, and what kind of young people's program they have?

Instead of looking at the social and economic factors as Jacob did, the question of paramount importance should be, What will this do for our spiritual lives? What effect will the schools, peer groups, and social climate have on our children?

Jacob settled for what suited him and found it to be morally disastrous for his family.

BLESSING IN DISGUISE

In the midst of these trials, God reminds Jacob of the vow he had made at Bethel more than twenty years earlier. Seeing Jacob has not obeyed His former command to return to "his relatives," He now tells him to go to Bethel *and live there* (Gen. 35:1; comp. 28:18-22; 31:3). Jacob obeys, but after building an altar, moves on in search of better pasture for his flocks. En route for Ephrath (Bethlehem), Rachel begins labor. Her birth-pains are so intense that, in giving life to her second son, she dies (note Gen. 30:1).

Jacob erects a memorial to mark the last resting place of his beloved wife. In all the time that has elapsed since he first met her at the well outside Haran, his love for her has never wavered. And when he himself will reach the end of his earthly pilgrimage, his memory of her will be as keen and as poignant as ever (Gen. 47:7).

After the burial of Rachel, we read: *"Then Israel journeyed on . . ."* (Gen. 35:21). Such a change in names is significant. Could it be that Rachel had been hindering Jacob's spiritual growth all these years? Is it possible that he had been so taken up with her that he had had no time for God? Whatever the answer to these questions may be, the change from *Jacob* to *Israel* indicates that what God had been at pains to develop in Jacob's character is at last taking place. In his hour of sorrow he learns to put his confidence in the Lord.

It is with this combination of spiritual strength and heaviness of heart that Jacob finally returns to his aged father, Isaac (Gen. 35:27). Rebekah has also died and the two men, father and son, who had never been close before, now enjoy one another's love and fellowship.

OVERCOMING THE "I" IN ME

Of the many important principles of family living which can be drawn from the life of Jacob, *the most fundamental is overcoming self-centeredness.*

Those of us who are the most selfish are constantly striving to make up for what we feel we lack. We acquire possessions, do things to enhance our prestige, and are engaged in a constant struggle for power. *We* may describe our motives and activities in different ways, but when we pause to think about it, our desire for these things shows our external, or fleshly, orientation (Gal. 5:17).

The quest for possessions, prestige, and power is never ending. We are never satisfied. We never have enough. And the reason? The things we seek are not what we really need. The things that give meaning to life are internal. A healthy image of oneself that counteracts the tendency towards self-centeredness consists of (a) a feeling of belonging, or acceptance; (b) a sense of intrinsic worth, or value; and (c) an awareness of our ability, or competence. These three things bring us the satisfaction we all search for. These are also the very things God worked so hard to cultivate in Jacob.

Think for a moment of Jacob at Shechem. He so wanted to *belong* that he bought a piece of land and was prepared to overlook the rape of his daughter to gain acceptance.

Jacob also wanted prestige, the blessing of the first-born, to enhance his feeling of *worth*. He therefore resorted to trickery, lies and deception in order to obtain it.

And in an hour of weakness and fear, after he had fled from Esau, God appeared to him at Bethel and gave him an unconditional promise. Jacob's feeling of powerlessness was such that he added a condition to God's promise in order to secure God's help on his behalf (Gen. 28:20-22). He did this in order to feel secure and *confident.*

Jacob's search for meaning and satisfaction stemmed from his poor image of himself as a person.

How different it might have been, had he responded to the Lord and developed an internal, or spiritual, orientation (Gal. 5:16-17).

Because we share the same fallen, sinful, human nature as Jacob, we too need to appropriate the provision God has made available to us. Our selfishness—which is a result of our poor image of himself—can be corrected by availing ourselves of the benefits of our relationship with the different members of the Godhead. As we found in previous chapters God has, by His own action, given us everything that is necessary for living a truly good, meaningful life. By availing ourselves of His provision—by partaking of the divine nature—we can escape the corruption that is in the world through lust (2 Peter 1:4).

As children of God the Father (by faith in Jesus Christ), we are members of His family (1 John 3:1-2a). We are accepted by Him (Eph. 1:6). We belong. We no longer need to accumulate things to make up for what we sense we lack. All that He has made available to us in Christ.

When we receive God the Son, the Lord Jesus Christ, as our Savior, we are immediately given the "adoption of sons."[7] The blessings of His inheritance become ours (Rom. 8:17). The reality of all this contributes to our sense of worth (1 Peter 1:18, 19). We need no longer seek worldly honors, for nothing that earth can offer can compare with what Christ has given us.

And God the Holy Spirit indwells us. By means of His power He makes all the benefits of Christ's resurrection available to us (Eph. 2:5-6). Positionally we are "in the heavenlies" and, through His work in us, He can work out in our daily lives the salvation which has been imparted to us (Phil. 2:12-13). He is the One who strengthens, enlightens, and empowers us.

What more could we ask for? With such blessing—coming from the vitality of our union with the Godhead—there is no reason for us to have a poor image of ourselves. We can instead draw our identity from our relationship with the Godhead. And as the way we think about ourselves begins to change, our self-centeredness will be replaced by (a) God-centeredness and (b) other-directedness.

Interaction

Discuss Jacob's desire for possessions, prestige, or power in the following situations. Consider what alternate action he might have taken. (If you are meeting in a group assign each question to a segment of the group or a couple). Apply the principles of a healthy self-image to situations you either have faced or are facing.

1. His bartering with Esau for the latter's birthright (Gen. 25:27-34).
2. His stealing of the blessing Isaac intended for Esau (Gen. 27:1-29).
3. His bargaining with God (Gen. 28:10-22).
4. His haggling with Laban over his wages, and his subsequent strategy (Gen. 30:29-43).
5. His settling in Shechem (Gen. 34:1-17; 25-31. Notice the indictment of his sons in v. 31).

13

LOVES ME, LOVES ME NOT

Many homes have started in romance and ended in recrimination and wretchedness because neither husband nor wife had a loyalty higher and more controlling than his or her desires.
—Glenn B. Ogden

Genesis 29:31—30:24; 31:1-7, 14-35; 49:31

During the months Mark courted Olive, the people in the church Olive attended tried hard to persuade her to break off the engagement. "Mark isn't a Christian," they warned. "You'll be unequally yoked with an unbeliever. Think of your children. Their father's influence may turn them away from Christ, and they may be lost forever."

Olive knew all this. The people at church pretended to be concerned, but somehow Olive missed any feeling of tender solicitude when they spoke to her about Mark. And as with young girls before and since, she felt that she might win Mark to the Lord. Besides, he was so much fun to be with. She couldn't imagine life without him, nor could she think of him being married to someone else.

In due course Mark and Olive were married. They traveled a great deal, saw all the notable sights, and met all the important people. Two daughters came to bless their home. At first Olive would read the Bible and pray, but as time went by she slipped further and further away from the Lord. She and Mark had everything. God seemed so unnecessary.

Then tragedy struck. One of their daughters died. All of a sudden Mark's materialistic philosophy of life was found to be insufficient for the crisis they faced. " 'Livy," he said, "if it comforts you to pray, do so now—for both of us."

As Olive searched within her soul for *faith* to pray, the awful reality of her spiritual condition dawned on her. The confidence of God's presence she had once known, was gone. With tears of remorse she replied, "I can't Mark; I don't have the faith to pray."

WHEN TWO BECOME ONE

When two people marry, they bring to the marriage different attitudes, backgrounds, and abilities. They must recognize that they are both imperfect beings with assets in their personalities as well as liabilities. Only by means of a strong commitment to spiritual and personal growth can their areas of weakness be corrected.

Take Jacob for example. By the time he arrives at the home of Laban, certain patterns of thought and action have become well-established. He is already beginning to reap the results of his conniving ways. He is a fugitive and virtually penniless. How different it might have been had he lived as Isaac did, in *"the fear of the Lord."* Then, when the time came for him to choose a wife, he could have obtained camels for his journey. He could have arrived at the home of Laban laden with gifts. And Laban, after being suitably impressed with the wealth of Rebekah's son, would have exclaimed (as he did on a former occasion), *"The matter comes from the Lord; I cannot speak to you good or bad.* There is my sad-eyed daughter Leah over there. She'll make you a good wife. But if you prefer bright-eyed Rachel, please take her with my blessing" (cf., Gen. 29:16, 17).

If this had happened there would have been no deception on the wedding night, no fourteen years of labor, no polygamy, and no secret flight from his father-in-law. But sin has its consequences to the sinner and to those associated with him.

CLASSIFIED: UNSUITABLE

Rachel, the person Jacob chooses to be his wife, is beautiful and attractive. Unfortunately, from her conversations recorded in Genesis, we can only conclude that she was devoid of those inner qualities which should evoke the admiration of others. Jacob loves her with a lover's impetuosity, but there is nothing to indicate that she returned his affection. She is a carbon copy of her father Laban, and brings to her marriage his scheming, subtle, deceptive ways. And worst of all, she is an idolater. There can be very little doubt about the fact that she hindered the development of Jacob's faith. By marrying her, Jacob was linking himself with an unbeliever.

BLESSING IN DISGUISE

Rachel's older sister, Leah, seems fated to remain single. She is described as tender-eyed, and in a land where bright eyes are the acme of beauty, this characteristic alone is enough to condemn her to second place.

Leah, the older of Laban's daughters, knows what it is like to grow through youth and adolescence with the admiring glances of the young men turning always in her sister's direction. As marriageable age approaches, she becomes increasingly aware of the plainness of her appearance. How she longs for someone to take notice of her, love her, and allow her to love him in return. She has so much to offer and is so willing to give of herself, but no one seems to care. And in this "school of affliction" is nurtured those qualities of tenderness and affection that ultimately will make her a fine wife and mother.

THE RIVALS

When Jacob arrives at the home of Laban both sisters must have eyed him with interest. And they both probably entertain the fantasy of having him as their husband.

At the end of one month Jacob agrees to work for seven years in lieu of a dowry. At the end of this time Rachel is to be given to him in marriage.

Near Eastern customs of marriage are fascinating. In the absence of an agreement entered into by the parents, all a suitor had to do to obtain a wife was pay a stipulated dowry and claim his bride. The father could then give a feast, and after this lead his daughter to a room where the groom was waiting. Their cohabitation that night constituted them husband and wife.

Imagine Rachel's excitement as Jacob's years of service for her draw to a close. And think of how it must have thrilled her to hear Jacob confront her father and ask for her to be given to him (Gen. 29:21, comp. v. 18).[1] However, after the marriage feast, Leah is substituted for her sister and when Jacob learns of Laban's deception the next morning, it is too late. Leah had no power to oppose her father's will, nor indeed was she likely to resist him, for as the record shows, a deep love for Jacob had sprung up in her heart. And so, with her father's approval and having spent the night with Jacob, she is now regarded as his wife.[2]

Polygamy was widely practiced, and so to placate Jacob, Laban promises him Rachel at the end of the week of celebrations (Gen. 29:25-28). But how can he right the wrong done his daughter? Laban doesn't even try. He contents himself with the excuse that it is the practice in Aram to marry off the first-born before the younger. And both Rachel and Jacob are left to bear the wrong done them, thankful for only one thing, that at last they are together.

There can be little doubt but that the trials Jacob and Rachel encounter draw them closer together. The adverse circumstances in the home of Laban have the effect of strengthening their relationship. And this is the way we too, as modern couples, should confront the problems we face. But of far greater value is the spiritual dimension. By involving the Lord in our trials and difficulties, we can turn adversity into stepping stones that will lead to greater maturity.

CHILDREN, BANE OR BLESSING?

For a wife in the ancient Near East to have children was regarded as the most important thing in her life. And if she bore her husband a son this was certain to endear her to him all his days.

With this in mind, let us consider the first six or seven years of marriage for Leah and Rachel (Gen. 29:31—30:24). Let us also learn from their experiences how to handle the disappointments of life.

Rachel possesses her husband's love, while Leah is neglected. Yet, Rachel is "one of those women with nothing to recommend her but her beauty. Her conversations show her to be bitter, envious, quarrelsome, and petulant. The full force of her hatred is directed against Leah."[3]

When God sees Jacob's partiality for Rachel, He endeavors to teach him some lessons that will ease the tensions in the home. He allows Leah to conceive. From this time onwards her "biography" can be read in the names she gives her sons. She calls her first Reuben, "Behold, a son!" saying, *"Because the LORD has seen my affliction; surely now my husband will love me"* (Gen. 29:32). Her second is Simeon, "Hearing," and she exclaims *"Because the LORD has heard that I am unloved, He has therefore given me this son also"* (Gen. 29:33).

Her usage of the covenant name for God, *Yahweh* (LORD), identifies her as a believer.

Hope dies hard in the human heart, and when Leah's third son, Levi, arrives she exclaims optimistically, *"This time my husband will become attached to me because I have borne him three sons"* (Gen. 29:34). But between the births of Levi and Judah a change takes place. Leah despairs of ever winning Jacob's love. With the arrival of her fourth son, it is evident that she is drawing on the Lord for the comfort she needs (Gen. 29:34), and He becomes the source of her satisfaction.

Leah's experience demonstrates that the deprivations which frustrate the satisfaction of our natural hopes and longings may become "blessings in disguise", if they lead to a deeper trust in the Lord. Romans 8:28 is not a sop to the stricken heart, but a profound truth concerning eternal verities. To come into a relationship with God—one of intimate fellowship and simple trust—is the supreme privilege and ultimate purpose of life; and blessed is every factor contributing toward it, no matter how distasteful it may for a time seem to be.[4]

Of course, when Rachel sees Leah bear one son after another, she becomes *jealous* of her sister. Her words to Jacob are illustrative of her nature. *"Give me children, or else I die!"* (Gen. 30:1). How much she needed to learn that children are a gift of the Lord. It is therefore a mark of His grace, when having promised the seed (Gen. 28:13-14), He withholds the promise for a time until mother and father are both ready.

Rachel's self-centeredness comes out clearly in another incident. This one is recorded in Genesis 30:14-16. When Leah's son finds some mandrakes[5] in the field and brings them to his mother, Rachel bargains with Leah for them. She is aware of the supposed aphrodisiac properties of mandrakes and believes that they may cause her to conceive. Imagine her chagrin when, having traded Jacob to Leah for a night, it is Leah who conceives (Gen. 30:17).

THE RIGHT COMBINATION

From the experience of Rachel we learn that those who "seem to have everything" are not necessarily as content as we might like to believe. Certainly Rachel was not. She wanted still more. And unless she could have what she wanted, life wasn't worth living. She didn't realize that God was working behind the scenes in an attempt to bring her to Himself. He knew of her spiritual needs and wanted to meet them before committing children to her care.

The experience of Helen and Tom was similar to Rachel's. As a young couple "they had everything going for them"— good jobs, a beautiful home—all they needed to make their lives complete was a family. Finally, after several years of trying, Helen conceived. She and Tom were jubilant, so much so that they could hardly wait to tell their friends! But nine weeks later there were the tell-tale signs of a miscarriage. When Tom came into the office the morning after Helen lost the baby he was crushed.

But what began as a tragedy became a means of blessing. Tom and Helen began to realize their insufficiency. Their hearts were opened to receive the message of the gospel. In a short time they both put their trust in Christ and were saved. The years since then have been good ones for both of them. They now have three children of their own and a Christian home in which to rear them.

GOD IS GRACIOUS

In the course of time God considers Rachel's plight and she conceives (Gen. 30:22). When her son is born she names him

Joseph, meaning "Adding," and says, *"Lord, add to me another son!"* (Gen. 30:24).[6]

But why has God seemingly changed His purpose? If withholding children from her was designed to bring her to Himself, then why interrupt the process?

The answer to these questions seems to be twofold.

First, God acts in grace toward Rachel. He does not withhold blessings from her indefinitely. Seeing she has not responded appropriately to the test, He will use some other means to accomplish His purpose.

Second, the arrival of Joseph furthers His purpose for the family. Jacob's thoughts immediately turn homewards. It is as if the child he has been waiting for at long last has arrived. He remembers that the Lord had promised to give the land of Canaan to his descendants (Gen. 28:13b). God, therefore, allowed Rachel to conceive and bear a son to further His greater purpose for the family.

It should be noted, however, that there may be times in our lives when our desire for something is so strong and our prayers so intense that the Lord may relent. This is what happened to the Israelites when they wandered about in the desert after leaving Egypt. The Bible says, *"He gave them their request, but sent leanness to their soul"* (Ps. 106:15). How much better it is to pray earnestly for the things we feel we need, but in an attitude of submission to His will so that our prayers will be answered when He knows we are ready.

HOMEWARD BOUND

When Jacob and his family do leave Aram for Canaan, Rachel steals her father's teraphim (or household gods), and takes them with her. To her they represent spiritual communion with the unseen. But is this all? Is her act indicative solely of her pagan, superstitious nature, or is there something else implied by the theft of these gods?

While different people have advanced their theories, Rachel's conduct must be evaluated in the light of her basic desires and the religious practices of the times.

The worship of the Ashtaroth was rife throughout the ancient Near East. These figurines honored the various fertility goddesses. Their worship was supposed to bring about fruitful seasons, cause livestock to bear, and women to conceive.[7]

Rachel's theft of these teraphim seems to give evidence, not only of the fact that she was an idolator (as opposed to a true worshipper of *Yahweh*), but also that her hope of another son was bound up in the fertility cult.

But notice her irreligion. When Laban pursues Jacob and demands of him the return of his teraphim, Rachel hides them in her camel's saddle (Gen. 31:30-35). She then sits on the saddle and excuses herself for not rising by pleading ceremonial defilement (Lev. 13:19-23). But her contact with the idols would have made them unclean too! Apparently her religious understanding is so primitive that this basic fact of worship is not a part of her belief.

CROWN OF THORNS

After several delays, God finally appears to Jacob and commands him to return to Bethel (Gen. 35:1ff). Jacob realizes that the worship of the Lord is incompatible with the idolatrous practices of some members of his household. He therefore commands that all teraphim be brought to him. These he buries under a tree. And with his family and servants having turned their backs on these false forms of belief, they make their way to Bethel.

At Bethel Jacob builds an altar to the Lord, and he and his wives and their children worship *Yahweh,* the God of his fathers, there.

Does this event mark the conversion of Rachel? It would seem so. The majority of commentators favor this view.

As they journey on from Bethel, Rachel begins labor (Gen. 35:16-20). As her life is slipping from her, she names her son Benoni, *"son of my sorrow."* It seems as if even this closing scene bears the impress of her egotism. She has spent all her energies over the years striving for control. Now, when faced with a situation she cannot govern, she turns in bitterness on the unwitting cause of her trial and vents her disappointment on him. She had demanded a son of the Lord following the birth of Joseph (Gen. 30:24), and now that He has given him to her, she shows her resentment by calling him Benoni.

Even Jacob's love for Rachel and grief over his loss cannot overlook this selfish (and perhaps spiteful) choice of names. He changes his son's name to Benjamin, which means *"son of my right hand."*

Rachel is the first woman mentioned in Scripture to die in childbirth (comp. 1 Tim. 2:15), and later writers use her sufferings as a symbol of the travail of the nation (Jer. 31:15; Matt. 2:18). She is not buried in the cave of Macpelah even though it is only a few hours journey away. Instead, she is buried near Bethlehem, and Jacob and his family then journey on to Hebron.

With Rachel's passing, Leah is the one who takes Benjamin to her heart and tenderly kisses away Joseph's tears. She lovingly rears her sister's sons, and it is probable that from this time onwards she begins to fill the vacuum in Jacob's life. And through her son Judah—the son whose birth marked the turning of her thoughts and hopes Godward—she becomes a direct ancestor of the Lord Jesus Christ.

In the course of time, when Leah dies, she is laid to rest in the cave of Macpelah with Abraham and Sarah, Isaac and Rebekah. And when Jacob passes away, his remains are laid next to hers (Gen. 49:29-31).

While temporal blessings of her life may have been few, the respect paid her in her death assures her an honored place in the annals of her people.

OVERCOMING LIFE'S VICISSITUDES

We all face life's inequities. Loneliness, neglect, deprivation, exploitation, or loss become a part of our experience at one time or another. When faced with situations such as these we find ourselves in the same kind of predicament Leah and Rachel faced. They both had cause to turn to the Lord in their need and obtain help from Him. Rachel had been wronged by her father, and in spite of all her efforts, remained childless. She could have turned to the Lord, but did not. Leah did, and found Him to be considerate whereas Jacob was neglectful. She experienced Him to be gracious while Rachel was envious and unrelenting in her hostility. And His loving-kindness sustained her when she and her sons were continuously relegated to second place.

The lessons of this story provide the answer to the problem of the deprivations and difficulties which overshadow the lives of so many. The inequalities of natural gifts and graces, of status and possessions, are seemingly so unfair to the underprivileged that if this life were all, then it would be impossible to believe that God is love. As Paul frankly declares, *"If in this life only we have faith in Christ, we are of all men most pitiable"* (1 Cor. 15:19). But since life is only the prelude for eternity, then we may well go on to say with the apostle, *"I reckon that the sufferings of this present time are not worthy to be compared with the glory which shall be revealed in us"* (Rom. 8:18; comp. 2 Cor. 4:17, 18; 1 Peter 1:6, 7).

The worldly-minded despise this doctrine and scornfully dismiss it. But those of us who are taught of God find in this truth not only the explanation of seeming unfairness in the government of the universe, but also the greatest incentive to faith and hope and love. It comforts our hearts and provides in countless practical ways the antidote to loneliness, fear, neglect, deprivation and oppression. The Lord becomes more than a doctrine. He is a person with whom we can fellowship and who not only cares for us, but who also helps us in *all* of life's situations. The vitality of our relationship with the Lord is in direct proportion to our sense of fulfillment. He becomes the source of our personal satisfaction, and this determines the extent to which we are able to meet the needs of our husband or wife, and our children.[8]

Interaction

1. Marriage is for *companionship*. This was God's plan (Gen. 2:18). Sin, however, often blights our relationships. What may a husband or wife do to cultivate the companionship of the one they married? Illustrate your conclusions with examples from the relationships covered in this book, or dealt with elsewhere in Scripture. How may these principles apply to your marriage?
2. Marriage provides the arena in which *love* develops and matures. In what ways is the biblical model in contrast to "Madison Avenue" journalism or "Hollywood-style" entertainment?

3. Marriage provides the setting for satisfying *sexual fulfillment*. Why has sexual perversion become what it is today (Gen. 6; Rom. 1:18ff.; etc.)? What was God's original intention? How do the relationships of couples in the book of Genesis illustrate either the benefits or the abuse of this God-given benefit? What are you able to learn from this analysis?

4. Marriage provides the means for the *perpetuation of the race*. Make a list of the respective and overlapping responsibilities of each parent. How do these contribute to the growth and development of a child? How well are you fulfilling your responsibilities? In what specific ways may you and your spouse work on areas of possible weakness?

5. Marriage provides a climate for *personal* (mental, moral, emotional) *and spiritual growth* of the couple. In what ways may Adam and Eve, Abraham and Sarah, Isaac and Rebekah, Jacob, Rachel and Leah have exerted (a) a positive, and (b) a negative influence on each other. How may we learn from their experiences? What are your areas of greatest weakness? Develop a plan whereby you and your husband or wife may help each other achieve greater maturity.

NOTES

CHAPTER 1

1. Experts now agree that "the greatest number of unhappy marriages and divorces occur among the ill-informed, the immature, and the over-indulged." See *Fraternity Monitor,* 1973.
2. We reject the view of Dr. Harold J. Ockenga that "regardless of whether God used dust of the ground or whether He used an animal whom He had already created [to make man], He bridged the gap by breathing into man the breath of life." *Women Who Made Bible History* (Grand Rapids: Zondervan Publishing House, 1962), p. 12.
3. Genesis 2 comes as a natural sequence to the events recorded so briefly in chapter 1. In Genesis chapter 1 man comes at the end of God's creative work. In chapter 2 he comes at the beginning as the commencement of human history. The two chapters are not antithetical, but supplementary. Each contains what the other lacks.
4. See H. C. Leupold, *Exposition of Genesis* (Grand Rapids: Baker Book House, 1960), I: 130-32.
5. These principles have been enlarged upon in Cyril J. Barber's "What is Marriage?" *Journal of Psychology and Theology,* II, 1 (Winter, 1974), 48-60.

CHAPTER 2

1. L. S. Chafer, *Systematic Theology* (Dallas: Dallas Seminary Press, 1947), II: 202-03; L. T. Talbot, *God's Plan of the Ages* (Grand Rapids: Eerdmans, 1936), pp. 23-24.
2. See John 8:44; 2 Corinthians 11:3; Revelation 12:9; 20:2. Compare Romans 16:20 and Genesis 3:15. It is evident from the curse placed upon the serpent that, at the time of the temptation, it must have stood erect (Gen. 3:14).
3. Satan uses the general word for God, *Elohim,* not the specific term "LORD God" found in chapter 2. See Leupold, *Exposition of Genesis,* I: 143.
4. Tradition claims that the forbidden "fruit" was an apple. For a full discussion see A. C. Custance, *The Virgin Birth and the Incarnation.* The Doorway Papers (Grand Rapids: Zondervan, 1976), V: 76-114.
5. In Genesis 1:28 God told Adam and Eve to "be fruitful and multiply, and fill the earth." From this statement some have concluded that Adam and Eve enjoyed Eden for less than nine months. The reasoning behind this view is that Eve is sure to have conceived during this time and, because no child is mentioned, their stay in the Garden must have been *less* than nine months. Genesis 1:28, however, should be interpreted as God's general intent. No haste is implied. He gave the same command to Noah and his wife after the flood (Gen. 9:1). Noah, we know, died without having sired any more children (Gen. 9:18, 19; comp. 6:9 and 10:1-32). While it is God's general intention that a married couple have children, He

has in times past withheld children from certain couples for specific purposes (Gen. 11:30; 20:8; 29:31; 30:2, 9, 17, 22; Judg. 13:2, 3; 1 Sam. 1:5, 6; etc.) Belief that Genesis 1:28 expresses God's general intention finds support in R. Patai's *Family, Love and the Bible* (London: Macgibbon & Kee, 1960), p. 64. The Bible also affirms that Cain was conceived *after* Adam and Eve were expelled from the Garden (Gen. 4:1); and Adam was 130 years old when Seth was born (Gen. 5:3). Allowing for the fact that both Cain and Abel were grown men at the time Abel was murdered, there seems to be ample time—say 75 or more years—during which Adam and Eve enjoyed Eden and before Cain was born. This would also be time enough for them (even in an idyllic situation) to begin to drift apart.

6. Why did Eve feel naked? And what does this have to do with us today? L. T. Talbot, in his excellent little book *God's Plan of the Ages* (pp. 22-29), claims that in the fall Eve (and subsequently Adam as well) lost the moral image of God. He believes that part of the divine image in which Adam and Eve were created included a raiment of light (Ps. 104:1, 2). This idea is later alluded to by the Lord Jesus in Matthew 22:11-13, and enlarged upon by the apostle Paul in his teaching of imputed righteousness (Rom. 3:22, 25; 4:3-5, 11-13, 22; 5:17; etc.). Those who practice public nudity today do more than attempt to turn back the clock to pre-Fall conditions. They vainly pretend (with their supposedly "enlightened" abandonment) to be free from sin. Nudity is, in reality, a revolt against God, for God's Word tells us that clothing was a felt need as soon as Adam and Eve sinned. God Himself made clothing for Adam and Eve. Nakedness and clothing are as inseparably connected as the fact of sin and the need of redemption.

7. See D. G. Barnhouse, *The Invisible War* (Grand Rapids: Zondervan, 1965), pp. 213-19.

CHAPTER 3

1. *Time* (Aug. 23), 1976. p. 32. The whole incident bears a striking parallel to the incident recorded in 2 Samuel 14:4-7.

2. Some evidence for Adam and Eve's training of Cain and Abel may be found in their relationship with God (in the system of sacrifices, Gen. 4:3-5), in their usage of the name *Yahweh,* LORD (not *Elohim,* God), and in their son's awareness of God (Cain talked with Him, vv. 6-15).

3. A euphemistic expression for sexual intercourse. Its usage in Genesis 4 in no way precludes the idea of previous intimacy but probably forms the basis of what has unfortunately come to be known as "carnal knowledge" with the accompanying tendency to equate sex with man's lower nature (i.e., with sin).

4. See Exodus 13:8-10; 20:12; Deuteronomy 4:9-10; 6:6-9; 11:19-20; 31:12-13; Psalm 78:1-8; Proverbs 1:8-9; 3:1-10; 4:1-4, 10-11, 20-22; 6:20-25; 22:6; 23:22; Isaiah 28:9-10; Joel 1:3; Ephesians 6:1-4; etc.

5. Those who see in the diversity of occupation, justification for the conflict between agricultural and pastoral ways of life—conflict common in the ancient Near East (see J. B. Pritchard's *Ancient Near Eastern Texts,* pp. 41-42)—ignore God's tacit approval of an agrarian economy found in Genesis 3:17-19.

6. A totally new, cultic explanation has recently been advocated by Rabbi H. Hirsch Cohen, in *The Drunkenness of Noah* (University, AL: University of Alabama Press, 1974), pp. 78-79, 85-89.

7. An analysis of Cain's rejection may be found in the work by C. J. Barber and J. D. Carter, *Always a Winner* (Glendale, CA: Gospel Light Publications, 1977), pp. 44-45.

8. In commenting on "In the course of time . . .", Gen. 4:3, Rabbi Cohen says, "Such a phrase, while not enumerating the exact amount of time that had elapsed,

conveys the impression that a lengthy span of time had passed. Thus the narrator was able to establish the fact that sufficient time had elapsed for the world's population to have increased from the first man and woman to such numbers that God needed an agent to remind people of the terms of the covenant. . . ." (*The Drunkenness of Noah,* p. 72; see also pp. 95-96).

9. Two books enlarge upon the need each one of us feels to be inwardly secure. They are by Maurice E. Wagner, and bear the titles *Put It All Together* and *The Sensation of Being Somebody* (Grand Rapids: Zondervan, 1974 and 1975).

CHAPTER 4

1. Certain versions translate this verse "What can the Almighty do *to us*?" While the translation we have used is to be preferred, both concepts show the contemptuous attitude of these people.
2. The emphasis on Enoch's example is unmistakable. Twice in these few verses it mentions his walk with God. This "walk" implied *agreement* (Amos 3:3), *obedience* (comp. Jer. 7:23), and *purpose* or direction (Prov. 3:5-6).
3. A "mystery" is not something mysterious but a truth concealed in Old Testament times and revealed in the New Testament (comp. Col. 1:26).

CHAPTER 5

1. (Grand Rapids: Zondervan, 1963), pp. 147-84; see also H. C. Leupold, *Exposition of Genesis* (Grand Rapids: Baker, 1960), I, 249ff.; and W. H. G. Thomas, *Genesis, a Devotional Commentary* (Grand Rapids: Eerdmans, 1966), pp. 65-74; etc.
2. C. Fred Dickason, *Angels: Elect and Evil* (Chicago: Moody, 1975), pp. 222-27; Merrill F. Unger, *Biblical Demonology* (Wheaton: Scripture Press, 1952), pp. 17-20, 46-49.
3. (London: Pickering & Inglis, 1970). Other writers who adhere to this theory are B. L. Ramm, *The Christian View of Science and Scripture* (Grand Rapids: Eerdmans, 1954); and W. U. Ault, "Flood (Genesis)" *Zondervan's Pictorial Encyclopedia of the Bible* (Grand Rapids: Zondervan, 1975), II: 550-63.
4. (Philadelphia: Presbyterian and Reformed, 1961). Other reputable writers espousing the universality of the deluge include Gleason L. Archer, Jr., *A Survey of Old Testament Introduction* (2d. ed.; Chicago: Moody, 1974), pp. 129-30, 202-11; and Paul A. Zimmerman, ed., *Rock Strata and the Biblical Record* (St. Louis: Concordia, 1970); etc. The last named work provides an important corrective to Ault's theory which is based on Carbon 14 dating. This system of dating materials is only accurate within observable limits and cannot be used to support a chronology before 1500 B.C. For the text of the famous Gilgamesh Epic see *Ancient Near Eastern Texts,* pp. 60-72.
5. The Hebrew of v. 9 is most interesting. *Tsadiq,* trans. "righteous," and *tamim,* "blameless," look at Noah's Godward and manward relationships. His separation to the Lord preserved him from the defilement all about him and kept his contact with those about him in perspective. His life before his contemporaries bore the fruit of his walk with the Lord.
6. See Arthur C. Custance, *Noah's Three Sons,* Vol. I: The Doorway Papers (Grand Rapids: Zondervan, 1975).
7. For information on the "waters which were above the earth" (Gen. 1:6, 7; 7:11) see J. C. Whitcomb, Jr., *The Early Earth* and *The World That Perished* (Grand Rapids: Baker, 1972 and 1973).

CHAPTER 6

1. Paul Tournier, *The Meaning of Persons* (New York: Harper & Row. 1957), pp. 12-13.
2. Those desirous of reading a biography on the life of Abraham are referred to F. B. Meyer's *Abraham: The Friend of God* (Fort Washington: Christian Literature Crusade, n.d.); historical information may be found in the excellent work by Leon Wood, *A Survey of Israel's History* (Grand Rapids: Zondervan, 1970), pp. 27-64; and the finest devotional commentary for lay readers is W. H. Griffith Thomas' *Genesis* (Grand Rapids: Eerdmans, 1966), specifically pp. 112-222.
3. Abraham was not the oldest son of Terah even though his name is mentioned first in Genesis 11:27-28.

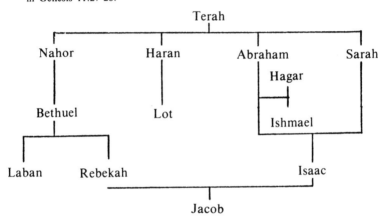

See H. C. Leupold, *Exposition of Genesis,* I: 397-99.
4. James L. Kelso in *Archaeology and Our Old Testament Contemporaries* (Grand Rapids: Zondervan, 1966), pp. 18-20, claims that Abraham was a "merchant prince." He believes that the etymology of *Habiru* (Hebrew) means "merchant." While Abraham left Haran with all their possessions (including camels, etc.), they did not actually become cattle and sheep farmers until after Abraham returned from Egypt (Gen. 12:10ff.; comp. 13:1-2). See also Cyrus H. Gordon, *Journal of Near Eastern Studies,* XVII (1958), pp. 28-31.
5. See C. Edwards' translation of *The Hammurabi Code* (Fort Washington: Kennikat, 1971), No's 146-47. Giving a servant to one's husband in order to have children was a common, legal practice in the ancient Near East. See also Genesis 30:1-13.

CHAPTER 7

1. See D. R. Mace, *Success in Marriage* (Nashville: Abingdon, 1958), p. 29.
2. *Ancient Near Eastern Texts,* p. 446.
3. Sarah was about sixty-five years old at the time. In view of the fact that she lived to one hundred and twenty-seven (Gen. 23:1), she was probably as beautiful then as a woman of thirty would be today. Incidental confirmation of this (as well as tacit confirmation of the great love Abraham had for Sarah) comes from the Dead Sea Scrolls. A scroll from Cave I contains an allusion to Abraham. Because it is not part of the inspired Scriptures, it has been called the *Genesis Apocryphon.* Here is a translation of a part of it:

"How beautiful is Sarai:
Her long, fine, glossy hair,
Her shining eyes, her charming nose,
The radiance of her face!
How full her breasts, how white her skin,
Her arms how goodly, how delicate her hands—
Their soft palms and long slender fingers—
How lissom her legs, how plump her thighs!
Of all virgins and brides
That beneath the canopy walk
None can compare with Sarai:
The fairest woman underneath the sky,
Excellent in her beauty;
Yet with all this she is sage and prudent,
. . ."

4. Making one's wife a "sister" was a part of Hurrian social custom. The Hurrians were a West Semitic branch of which the Patriarchs were a part. When a Hurrian husband made his wife his "sister" he immediately conferred on her the highest honor possible. As her "[blood] brother" he had the same kind of legal power over her that a father or the head of a household had over the members of the family. Such acts gave the woman the kind of protection she needed. Those not so honored tended to be treated as things rather than as people of worth. See E. A. Speiser, "The Wife-Sister Motif in the Patriarchal Narratives," *Biblical and Other Studies* (Waltham, MA: Brandeis University, 1962), I:15-28. We have no sure means of knowing whether or not Abraham was influenced by this Hurrian custom.

5. W. G. Blaikie, *Heroes of Israel* (London: T. Nelson, 1894), pp. 56-57.

6. R. de Vaux, *Ancient Israel*, pp. 26-33; D. R. Mace, *Hebrew Marriage* (London: Epworth, 1953), pp. 24-27, 169-174.

7. There is in the British Museum an ancient Egyptian papyrus which, although of a later date than the time of Abraham, proves that his fears on entering Egypt were not groundless. This papyrus relates how a Pharaoh, on the advice of his counselors, sent armies to take away a man's wife and murder her husband.

8. For an analysis of fear as well as how to handle it, see C. J. Barber, *Searching for Identity* (Chicago: Moody, 1975), pp. 120-132; and his discussion of "the fear of the LORD" in *Nehemiah and the Dynamics of Effective Leadership* (Neptune, NJ: Loizeaux, 1976), pp. 70-72, 88-93.

9. Archaeologists have identified these kings. They represented the mightiest nations of their day. See W. F. Albright, "Abraham the Hebrew," *Bulletin of the American Society for Oriental Research*, 163 (1961), 36-54; and *Archaeology, Historical Analogy and Early Biblical Tradition* (Baton Rouge, LA: Louisiana State University Press, 1966), pp. 26f.

10. Meekness is wrongly equated with weakness. These terms are *not* synonymous. The essence of meekness is *bridled strength.*

CHAPTER 8

1. Gary H. Strauss, "What Really Happened in Eden?" *Psychology for Living*, XVII, 12 (December, 1976), pp. 18-19.

2. The visit of these "travellers" has led certain segments of the Christian church to see in their number a foreshadowing of the doctrine of the Trinity. This even was certainly a personal manifestation of God in visible form (Gen. 18:13-14, 22).

3. L. M. Epstein, *Marriage Laws in the Bible and the Talmud* (Cambridge: Harvard University Press, 1942), pp. 8, 56-7; R. de Vaux, *Ancient Israel,* pp. 24-25, 41; D. D. Luckenbill, "The Code of Hammurabi," *The Origin and History of Hebrew Law* (Chicago: University of Chicago Press, 1931).
4. See C. J. Barber and G. H. Strauss, *Your Children Have Real Possibilities* (San Bernardino, CA: Here's Life, 1980).
5. For a discussion of this kind of manipulative technique, see Eric Berne's book *Games People Play* (New York: Grove Press, 1966).
6. For an analysis of how infidelity arises, see O. Quentin Hyder's *The People You Live With* (Old Tappan: Revell, 1975), pp. 163-175.
7. This term is used to describe the reasons why a husband or a wife may refrain from sex or use sexual gratification as a lever to get their own way. John Scanzoni deals with this destructive phenomenon in *Sexual Bargaining: Power Politics in the American Marriage* (Englewood Cliffs: Prentice-Hall, 1972). See 1 Corinthians 7:2-5 (RSV).

CHAPTER 9

1. Adapted from J. B. Phillip's translation so as to bring out the contrast of the Greek text. It is interesting to note that the Greek word translated "adorn" in verses 3 and 5 is one from which we derive the word cosmetic.
2. L. M. Epstein, *Marriage Laws in the Bible and the Talmud,* pp. 19, 32-33, 293-94; D. R. Mace, *Hebrew Marriage,* pp. 202-05, 210-12.
3. H. V. Morton, *Women of the Bible* (London: Metheun, 1964), pp. 19-20. Italics added.
4. First Samuel deals with this theme. For a concise explanation see the book by C. J. Barber and J. D. Carter, *Always a Winner* (Glendale, CA: Gospel Light, 1977). See also *Searching for Identity* (Chicago: Moody, 1975), pp. 32-40.
5. C. H. Gordon, *Journal of Near Eastern Studies,* XVII, I, 30.
6. *Buried History,* II (November, 1965), pp. 15-16. See also "The Code of Hammurabi," No. 145.

CHAPTER 10

1. W. K. Lacey, *The Family in Classical Greece* (Ithaca, NY: Cornell University Press, 1968), p. 197.
2. There were three primary words for love used by the Greeks: *eros,* "sensual love;" *philia,* "tender affection;" and *agapē,* "a sincere heart-felt concern that manifests itself in desiring the highest good in the one loved." By comparison our English word "love" fails to convey what we mean and needs qualification. It is *agapē* love that a husband should show his wife (Eph. 5:25). It emanates from the will, not the emotions (although emotion need not be excluded), and is a manifestation of the fruit of the Spirit (Gal. 5:22).
3. M. Burrows, *The Basis of Israelite Marriage* (New Haven, CT: American Oriental Society, 1938); E. Neufeld, *Ancient Hebrew Marriage Laws,* pp. 94-117.
4. *The Babylonian Talmud,* Yebamoth, 28, 393f., 738, 746; Ketuboth, 271, 266f., 618f. A young childless widow might return to her father's home and remarry after a period of time (e.g., Gen. 38:11; Ruth 1:8, 9). She might also be claimed in marriage by her late husband's brother (Gen. 38:8; Ruth 1:12ff.; Mark 12:19ff.); or her nearest kinsman (Deut. 25:5; Ruth 3:12, 13).
5. W. H. Griffith Thomas, *Genesis,* p. 224.
6. Oscar Wilde, in "The Importance of Being Earnest" (Act 1), has an interesting comment on the influence of mothers. "All women become like their mothers. That is their tragedy. *No man does. That's his.*" Perhaps Isaac was an exception. (Italics added.)

7. Abraham lived to be 175. In all probability *he* likened the famine to the one he remembered when he and Sarah first entered Canaan. He may have been the one who suggested to Isaac that he go either to Egypt or Philistia (comp. Gen. 26:2).

8. When Isaac went to Gerar he feared the people there and said of Rebekah, "She is my sister." Had he continued to "fear" the Lord (i.e., hold God as the object of his reverence) he would have been kept from telling a lie and practicing deception. For the believer, God is the proper fear-Object. Reverence for Him and doing His will should preclude other fears. In Isaac's case (as well as in ours, when other people put us in fear), the Philistines became an improper fear-object. In feeling threatened by what they might do to him, Isaac experienced fear-conflict—an inner struggle between what he should and should not do. He attributed to these Philistines two prerogatives of God: almightiness and impendency (the power to harm him). And he succumbed to fear because his trust in the Lord had momentarily been eclipsed by his fear of man.

9. Never again in Scripture do we read of Rebekah saying a kind word to Isaac. It is no wonder that with his health declining and his eye-sight fading he should place his love in the only one who was kind to him: Esau. For an example of how Rebekah might have handled her anger see "Anger, and How to Handle it" in *Nehemiah and the Dynamics of Effective Leadership,* pp. 83-87.

10. See the "Psychology of Good Questions" in *Nehemiah and the Dynamics of Effective Leadership,* pp. 34-36.

11. Isaac was God's theocratic representative on earth. To him had been given the power to act on God's behalf. This fact is illustrated for us in several ways, notably in (a) Abimelech's attitude towards Isaac, and (b) in the power Isaac possessed to impart either blessings or cursings. Note first that Abimelech recognized his greatness and, following the death of Abraham (with whom there had been a treaty), came to Isaac suing for peace. Second, Jacob was cognizant of his father's special power and feared to do as his mother suggested (Gen. 27:12b). The blessing of Isaac was more than just the deathbed wishes of an old man. The benediction he pronounced would come to pass (note Gen. 27:33) just as if God Himself had spoken it. See A. C. Schultz, "Theocracy," *Zondervan's Pictorial Encyclopedia of the Bible,* V: 718-19. For a full explanation of the theocratic concept in the Old Testament see Alva J. McClain's excellent book *The Greatness of the Kingdom* (Chicago: Moody, 1954).

CHAPTER 11

1. Interested parties should read Helen B. Andelin's book *Fascinating Womanhood* (Rev. ed.; Santa Barbara, CA: Pacific Press, 1975), and husbands are referred to the equally good work by Aubrey P. Andelin, *Man of Steel and Velvet* (Santa Barbara, CA: Pacific Press, 1972).

2. For the significance of the gifts see D. R. Mace, *Hebrew Marriage,* pp. 24-27; and E. Neufeld, *Ancient Hebrew Marriage Laws* (London: Longmans, Green & Co., 1944), pp. 94-117.

3. P. Tournier, *To Understand Each Other* (Richmond, VA: John Knox Press, 1968), pp. 31-33. See also the book by D. H. Small, *After You've Said "I Do"* (Old Tappan, NJ: Fleming H. Revell, 1968), for helpful ways to communicate in marriage.

4. L. M. Epstein, *The Jewish Marriage Contract,* p. 207; and *Marriage Laws in the Bible and the Talmud,* pp. 23, 27, 32-33, 293-94; also E. Neufeld, *Ancient Hebrew Marriage Laws,* pp. 118-134.

5. The material here has been adapted from John Powell's book *Why Am I Afraid to Tell You Who I Am?* (Chicago: Argus Communication, 1969).

6. See H. A. Ironside, *Addresses on First Corinthians* (Neptune, NJ: Loizeaux Bros., 1952), pp. 417-32.
7. Some indication of Esau's feelings of rejection may be seen in his intense desire to please his parents after Jacob has been sent away to obtain a wife from "the daughters of Laban" (Gen. 28:2). He seeks out Ishmael, the son of Abraham, Isaac's father, and marries one of his daughters (Gen. 28:6-9).

CHAPTER 12

1. Neufeld, *Ancient Hebrew Marriage Laws,* pp. 94-117.
2. See E. M. Duvall, *Family Development* (Philadelphia: Lippincott, 1971), p. 78.
3. *Genesis: A Devotional Commentary,* p. 277. H. V. Morton, in *Women of the Bible* comments on the characters of this tragic story. Of Jacob he says, "There is no doubt in my mind that his character was ruined by his mother, Rebekah. . . ." Then he continues:

> Leah loved Jacob. There is no indication that Rachel loved him as much. . . .
> Running through this love story is a strange sub-plot. Jacob, the man of wits, met his match in Laban. Laban was a greedy, dishonest man, and it seems that, in encountering his dishonesty and suffering his deception, Jacob was paying the penalty for having stolen his brother's birthright. At the end of his seven years' labour Jacob was tricked into marriage with Leah. She is the most tragic figure in the drama. She genuinely loved her husband; but still his eyes and his mind turned always to her sister.
> Rachel, even after marriage with Jacob, remains one of those women with nothing to recommend but beauty. She is bitter, envious, quarrelsome and petulant. The full force of her hatred is directed against her sister, Leah (pp. 40, 42).

4. Dr. J. Gresham Machen expressed this principle in national terms: *"America is running on the momentum of a godly ancestry. When that momentum goes, God help America!"* (Italics added).
5. Thomas, *Genesis,* p. 277.
6. The same Hebrew word used to describe the rape of Dinah is used of the desecration of the Temple (Ezek. 23:38).
7. See John Murray's article on "Adoption," in *Baker's Dictionary of Theology* (Grand Rapids: Baker, 1960), pp. 25-26.

CHAPTER 13

1. To "go in" to a woman was a euphemistic expression for sexual intercourse. Such an act conducted "before witnesses" (who obviously were not present in the room) but saw the father take the bride to the room where the groom was waiting, constituted marriage (Gen. 29:23).
2. If pressed by Jacob, Laban (who was a most deceitful man) could always claim that the seven years of service was for one of his daughters, not necessarily Rachel. To have the marriage annulled would have had disastrous repercussions on Leah. It would imply that Jacob had found her virginity had been violated (Deut. 22:13-21) and it would have been impossible for her ever to have secured

another husband. In going along with her father's plans, Leah took considerable risk. See Mace, *Hebrew Marriage*, pp. 178-83; de Vaux, *Ancient Israel*, pp. 27, 33-35; Neufeld, *Ancient Hebrew Marriage Laws*, pp. 89-93.

3. *Women of the Bible*, p. 42.
4. See H. F. Stevenson, *A Galaxy of Saints* (London: Marshall, Morgan & Scott, 1957), p. 27.
5. See R. K. Harrison, "The Mandrake and the Ancient World," *The Evangelical Quarterly* (1977), 87-92.
6. The Hebrew *yosêf* is usually translated as a Jussive, "May the Lord add. . . ." The form of the verb is better taken as a Hiphil Imperfect implying causation and intensifying the action.
7. Y. Aharoni, *The Land of the Bible* (Philadelphia: Westminster Press, 1962), pp. 50-51, 159ff.
8. Stevenson, *A Galaxy of Saints*, p. 30.

A Companion Volume

YOU CAN HAVE A HAPPY MARRIAGE

If marriage was "divinely instituted for the benefit of mankind", what has gone wrong? Are you languishing in an unhappy marriage? And what can be done to make your marriage happy?

In *You Can Have a Happy Marriage*, a sequel to *Your Marriage Has Real Possibilities*, Cyril J. and Aldyth A. Barber devote themselves to answering such questions. They have discovered from their extensive counseling ministry that numerous couples have borne out the importance of the kind of relationship mentioned in Genesis 2:24:

> For this cause a man shall leave his father and mother [*the need for maturity*], and cleave to his wife [*the need for unity*]; and they shall become one flesh [*the need for sexual compatibility*].

Through a series of special case studies of couples in the Bible, the authors endeavor to show that "marriages are successful where trust is honored, where views are shared, where companionship is treasured, and where love is given a chance to flow freely."

This unique study book, written in a very readable style, is ideal for individual or group use. The *Interaction* section at the close of each chapter will prove extremely valuable for you who seriously seek to follow a biblical example for a happy marriage.